D1365253

THE
LIVING STORY
OF THE
OLD TESTAMENT

Books by Walter Russell Bowie

THE STORY OF THE BIBLE

THE STORY OF THE CHURCH

LIFT UP YOUR HEARTS

CHRIST BE WITH ME

THE STORY OF JESUS FOR YOUNG PEOPLE

GREAT MEN OF THE BIBLE

THE MASTER: A LIFE OF JESUS CHRIST

I BELIEVE IN JESUS CHRIST

THE LIVING STORY OF THE NEW TESTAMENT

JESUS AND THE TRINITY

MEN OF FIRE

"In the beginning God created the heaven and the earth."

THE
LIVING STORY
OF THE
OLD TESTAMENT

by

Walter Russell Bowie

Illustrated by Douglas Rosa

PRENTICE-HALL, INC.
Englewood Cliffs, N.J.

Copyright Acknowledgment

The Scripture quotations printed in inset in this book, together
with some other brief quotations, are mostly from the Revised
Standard Version of the Bible, Copyright 1946, 1952, by the
Division of Christian Education, National Council of Churches.

PRENTICE-HALL INTERNATIONAL, INC., *London*
PRENTICE-HALL OF AUSTRALIA, PTY., LTD., *Sydney*
PRENTICE-HALL OF CANADA, LTD., *Toronto*
PRENTICE-HALL OF INDIA (PRIVATE) LTD., *New Delhi*
PRENTICE-HALL OF JAPAN, INC., *Tokyo*
PRENTICE-HALL DE MEXICO, S.A., *Mexico City*

To
JAMES MUILENBURG
*Inspired interpreter of the Old Testament's
meaning and its everlasting message.*

Foreword

THE PART of the Bible which is called the Old Testament comes down to us from very long ago. The scenes upon which men of the Old Testament times looked out have mostly vanished from the earth. Great cities whose names resounded in its history are now only echoes of the dead, and kingdoms and empires which were mighty then have crumbled into dust. But out of the ancient centuries one central fact continues. It is the story of a people who could not be destroyed—the people of Israel, who seemed little amongst the nations but whose greatness was that they had a covenant with God. So from their history have come the influences which most of all have lifted human life up toward what it ought to be: duty toward God and man made clear in the Ten Commandments; the high desires which can wake in every soul as the psalms have sung of them; the answer of conscience to the voices of the prophets preaching justice and mercy and devotion to the will of God. Therefore the story of the Old Testament is forever a *living* story, because it proclaims to every generation the high and holy purpose to which all men need to be alive.

WALTER RUSSELL BOWIE

Alexandria, Va.

Contents

CHAPTER ONE

What the Old Testament Is

THE BOOKS in the Bible, beginning with the Book of Genesis, that make up the Old Testament were written a long time ago. The latest of them are more than two thousand years old, and most of them are hundreds of years older than that. The story they tell belongs to ancient history, and deals with times and places that seem very far away. How, then, can the Old Testament be a *Living* Story?

Because, in the first place, it brings before us a succession of men and women so vivid that they seem to be forever alive. It is said that Oliver Cromwell exclaimed to the artist who was about to paint his official portrait, "Paint me as I am, wart and all." He wanted honesty, neither less nor more. And that is the way the Old Testament paints the figures who play their parts in its long history. There they are in their human genuineness and their infinite variety: Abraham, Isaac, Esau, Jacob, Joseph, Deborah and Moses, Saul and David, Samson and Delilah, the good and the bad and the in-between, the great and the small. When reading about them, one is not back in any particular age, but standing face to face with human nature as it always is. He is touching the everlasting reality of life.

And the Old Testament is also a Living Story because it is the history of an enduring people. Millenniums ago, in the heartland of Asia, the cradle of so much of civilized mankind, the Semitic race appeared. Out of it came the people that would be called the Hebrews, and "the Children of Israel"; and later, from the name of the strongest tribe, the tribe of Judah, they would be called the Jews. All through the centuries, in times of prosperity and in times of persecution, through temporary triumphs and in what sometimes seemed the last hopelessness of disaster, the people of Israel have kept their integrity and indomitable belief, so that nothing could destroy it.

The Old Testament is the revelation of what has made these people great. The record was not made all at once. Instead, it was the gradual accumulation of the experiences and the beliefs that reflected life through many centuries. Probably in the tenth century B.C., perhaps about the year 950, in the Kingdom that had been built by David and Solomon, some man whose name we may never know, but who was one of the great pioneers in literature, began to write down what he knew and what he could learn. He had immediate knowledge of what had happened in David's time and what was happening in the time of Solomon— the same King Solomon who built the immense stables for his chariot horses, the broken stalls of which have recently been uncovered in Palestine at Megiddo. The King Solomon who opened the copper mines which have been found and re-opened near the city of Elath on the Gulf of Aquabah. Parts of the Books of Samuel have the fresh and intimate detail of records that had just been written. But this man who was one of the first historians had an expansive idea of history. He also wanted to gather up all the ancient traditions that had been passed on by word of mouth from generation to generation. Some of these were stories that had been told around the camp fires of the desert tribes—stories that had to do with tribal names and customs and with special places, such as an oasis or some great tree or sheltering rock which had been the scene of legendary happenings. There were fragments of old battle songs and chants of triumph concerning some remembered hero. And there were the naive wonderings of early people concerning life and the world and God, and the folklore that had grown up with their religion. All this was woven into the story of Israel's past, and became the framework for much of the first part of the Old Testament, especially for the Book of Genesis.

That was the beginning. Then came another historian, a century or two later, who gathered all that he could learn about what had been thought and believed and told in ancient times. There were chronicles kept at the court of the kings and at the temple in Jerusalem. There were laws and regulations concerning worship drawn up by the priests. There were bursts of poetry, like the Book of Job, and the immortal utterances of joy and sorrow, of prayer and penitence, that make up the Book of Psalms. Then came the prophets, and their mighty messages were added to the great library which became the complete Old Testament.

So the Old Testament grew and expanded with the growth of a people's mind and soul, and in this sense too it is a Living Story.

But the greatest fact remains. If the Old Testament were only a record of human happenings, it could fade and be forgotten as the years go by. But it is never concerned with human happenings alone. Across the great stage of its narrative many figures move; but above the stage and all the figures on it is One unseen by mortal eyes, yet visible supremely to the eyes of faith. For the interpreters in Israel, the history of their people was not something bounded by the meanings of this earth. It was the story of the developing purpose of the living God.

God is the Lord of all nations, and therefore the history of each nation has something to teach about the working of his will. What makes the Old Testament different is that the people to whom it has belonged thought more of God, tried harder to be obedient to his Spirit, and so were inspired to express his truth more fully than any others in their world. Accordingly it has come to pass that the Bible is not only a story of yesterday, it is a living Word of guidance for all the days to come.

CHAPTER TWO

The Story of Creation

T HE BOOK of Genesis, with which the Old Testament opens, means the Book of the Beginnings.

Farther back than history goes, when men first began to think and wonder, they started to ask questions concerning their world and how it came to be. Who made the earth and the sky? What is man's destiny, and how is he different from the animals? And what is it, or Who is it, that men should know and worship?

In the ancient countries, and especially in Babylon, there were accounts of how men believed the world began. Some of these were crude mythologies of wars between hostile gods and goddesses, or between the gods and dragons, with half the body of a slain monster made into the earth and the other half into the sky. In other lands were other explanations: a cosmic egg by the banks of the Nile, according to Egyptians; or the limbs of a giant, according to some of the writings of the Indian Rigveda. No one would now think that those gropings toward understanding had expressed the actual facts; but in the dawn of human thinking men's minds were projecting their questions into the unknown, and coming back with such answers as their imaginations could conceive.

Alongside the myths of many peoples stands the account of the creation with which the Bible begins. It is different from those other stories—and important first of all is to see what the crucial difference is. Not in being "scientific." Men in ancient Israel could not anticipate, any more than other human beings could, the knowledge of the universe which has come through the patient thought and study of the centuries since. They could only draw the picture which their reverent imagination saw. But the difference was that their imagination had a spiritual discernment that was new. The details of their story of Creation could not go beyond conjecture; but the details, and the story as a whole, have the noble loftiness of the words that are the prelude, "In the beginning, God."

Then follows the description, as it had been shaped in the thought of the people of Israel, of how the universe was created. But it was not so much the how as the Who that mattered.

> The earth was without form and void, and darkness was upon the face of the deep; and the Spirit of God was moving over the face of the waters.
> And God said, "Let there be light"; and there was light. And God saw that the light was good; and God separated the light from the darkness. God called the light Day, and the darkness he called Night. And there was evening and there was morning, one day.

So, like a great poem and like a roll of organ music, the introduction to the Old Testament's story begins. On it goes, through the six days on which it was believed that the hands of God were working.

Though the light had dawned on the first day, still the waters of the great deep washed everywhere, and nothing else could be seen through the grey clouds. So God made the blue dome of the sky; and put the waters for the rain above it, and the waters of the sea below. And that was the second day.

Then out of the sea God made the land arise, with its mountains and hills, its valleys and meadows; and over all the earth he spread the green mantle of grass and trees and blossoming.

That was the third day; and on the fourth, God made the sun to shine by day and the moon to shine by night, and beyond the moon he spread the unnumbered stars.

But in the waters yet there was no living thing, nor anything on wings beneath the sky. So God made the fish in the sea and birds to fly in the air; and that was the work of his hands for the fifth day.

Meanwhile, the surface of the earth itself was quiet, and nothing moved upon the ground. Then God made the beasts and cattle to roam the forests and the fields.

And then on that same sixth day came God's final work.

> "Let us make man in our image, after our likeness," he
> said; "and let them have dominion over the fish of the sea,
> and over the birds of the air, and over the cattle, and over
> all the earth, and over every creeping thing that creeps
> upon the earth." So God created man in his own image, in
> the image of God he created him; male and female he cre-
> ated them. And God blessed them, and God said to them,
> "Be fruitful and multiply, and fill the earth and subdue
> it; and have dominion over the fish of the sea and over the
> birds of the air and over every living thing that moves on
> the face of the earth."
>
> Thus the heavens and the earth were finished, and all
> the host of them. And on the seventh day God finished his
> work which he had done, and he rested on the seventh day
> from all his work which he had done. So God blessed the
> seventh day and hallowed it.

Such was the picture of Creation—coming probably from priests
and scribes of the temple in Jerusalem some 2400 or 2500 years
ago—as they conceived the Creation to have been. And when they
wrote of God resting on the seventh day, they were putting the
seal of God himself on what had begun to be established as the
Sabbath Holy day of worship and of rest.

It is plain that we of today cannot think of Creation as the
Book of Genesis describes it. Time has brought knowledge which
men of the earlier ages could not have. The strata of the earth's
great rocks and the fossils in them show that it may have been
millions of years and not six days that the earth was in the making. Astronomers know that it was after, and not before, the sun
was made that this little world of ours appeared. As a time chart
and a scientific sequence, the account in Genesis is a long way
from the facts. But that does not touch the heart of its immortal
value. For the early part of Genesis was never meant to be sta-
tistical prose. It is worshipful imagination. The men who framed
it were expressing their fundamental faith: that this created universe came not from accident nor from any blind force and brutish-
ness, but from a God whose good purpose men can understand
and trust.

CHAPTER THREE

In the Garden of Eden

"G OD SAW every thing that he had made, and behold, it was very good." That is the way the priestly writers summed up their story of Creation—the story they put on the first page of the whole Bible. It stands there in a kind of finished dignity, like the proclamation of a creed.

But this notable fact about the Old Testament, and especially about the Book of Genesis, is that it is not all of one piece. As we have already remembered, the men who ultimately brought the materials of the Books together tried to save and put in everything that expressed their peoples' consciousness of God. They had no worried concern to make sure that whatever they included should fit into a consistent pattern. They were not writing arithmetic, where it is always necessary to have two plus two before it is possible to have four. They knew that it is *not* always necessary to use stiff, literal language in order to convey the truth. Folklore as well as history might express the one great fact which was to be the cardinal message of the Bible: what matters above everything is God. So, in the second chapter of Genesis there is another account of the Creation, which had floated down the stream of tradition from a far earlier time—when people lived in an age of marvels, and told what was real to them in stories and pictures, with the kind of spontaneous imagination which children use.

It could be true, as the first chapter of Genesis said, that "God saw everything that he had made, and behold, it was very good." But something had happened to the goodness. How had pain and suffering come in? Why does the lot of men and women sometimes seem so hard? And how did it happen that in human life there can be so much evil? Those are some of the questions that

7

men have brooded over since the beginning of time; and one of
their answers is the story of the Garden of Eden, and of the man
and the woman who were in its paradise and then were driven out.

> In the day that the Lord God made the earth and the
> heavens, when no plant of the field was yet in the earth
> and no herb of the field had yet sprung up—for the Lord
> God had not caused it to rain upon the earth, and there was
> no man to till the ground; but a mist went up from the
> earth and watered the whole face of the ground—then the
> Lord God formed man of dust from the ground, and
> breathed into his nostrils the breath of life, and man be-
> came a living being. And the Lord God planted a garden
> in Eden, in the east; and there he put the man whom he
> had formed. And out of the ground the Lord God made to
> grow every tree that is pleasant to the sight and good for
> food, the tree of life also in the midst of the garden, and
> the tree of the knowledge of good and evil.

So all the Garden belonged to the man whom God had made—
except one tree. That was the tree of the knowledge of good and
evil. It was commanded that the man should not eat of that, for
to eat of it would mean that he had lost his innocence and learned
the taste of wrong.

But the man had no companion in the Garden, and God said
"It is not good that the man should be alone; I will make him a
helper fit for him." So God made birds and beasts and brought
them to the man to see what he would call them. But none of them
could keep the man from feeling lonely. Then God caused a deep
sleep to fall upon the man, and he took one of his ribs and made
it into a woman, and brought her to the man. And the man said:

> This at last is bone of my bones
>   and flesh of my flesh;
> She shall be called Woman,
>   because she was taken out of Man.

God gave to the man the name of Adam, and to the woman the
name of Eve. And the man and his wife were both naked, and
were not ashamed.

But there was something else in the Garden that Adam and Eve would have to reckon with; and in the third chapter of the story in Genesis it appears.

> Now the serpent was more subtle than any other creature that the Lord God had made. He said to the woman, "Did God say, 'You shall not eat of any tree of the garden?' " And the woman said to the serpent, "We may eat of the fruit of the trees of the garden; but God said, 'You shall not eat of the fruit of the tree which is in the midst of the garden, neither shall you touch it, lest you die.' " But the serpent said to the woman, "You will not die. For God knows that when you eat of it your eyes will be opened, and you will be like God, knowing good and evil."

Very plausible that seemed to Eve, as the voice of temptation often does. There was the good fruit within reach upon the tree, seeming all the more alluring now because it had been forbidden. So she took of the fruit and ate of it, and she gave some of it to Adam, and he ate too.

> Then the eyes of both were opened, and they knew that they were naked.
> And they heard the sound of the Lord God walking in the garden in the cool of the day, and the man and his wife hid themselves from the presence of the Lord God among the trees of the garden. But the Lord God called to the man, and said to him, "Where are you?" And he said, "I heard the sound of thee in the garden, and I was afraid, because I was naked; and I hid myself." He said, "Who told you that you were naked? Have you eaten of the tree of which I commanded you not to eat?" The man said, "The woman whom thou gavest to be with me, she gave me fruit of the tree, and I ate." Then the Lord God said to the woman, "What is this that you have done?" The woman said, "The serpent beguiled me, and I ate."

So in the ancient story that in its overtones is so timeless, everybody wanted to blame somebody else. But God's truth stripped away the thin excuses and his judgment fell upon all concerned. The serpent should crawl in the dust and be feared and hated by all human beings. The woman should bring forth children in pain and the man should have to toil and sweat to earn his livelihood. The days in the paradise of Eden were finished. The Lord drove out the man and woman, and placed at the gate of the Garden an angel with a flaming sword, to bar them from coming back.

Thus the story gave what it thought were answers to some of the things that the early peoples wondered about: why men loathe snakes; why women must labor and suffer in childbirth; and why when they have planted seed they always have to struggle to keep it from being stifled by weeds and rank growth in the ground.

But over and above these particular matters, there was the ruling interest that possessed all those who brought together the history, the stories and the traditions that make up the Bible. From first to last they were concerned with God and his relationship to human life. In the story of the Garden of Eden there is expressed the everlasting truth that there is a Purpose higher than themselves that men must recognize; and when they try to forget and to disobey it, there will be disaster.

CHAPTER FOUR

When Evil Began to Spread

T HE TROUBLE that began in Eden did not stop there. Adam and
Eve had listened to the voice of evil. That voice would have
more, and worse, to say to the next generation.

So comes the story of Cain and Abel.

Cain and Abel were the sons of Adam and Eve, and they, like
Adam and Eve, were no longer in the Garden, where food could
be had for the taking. Abel was a keeper of sheep, but Cain was a
tiller of the ground. In the course of time, Cain brought to the
Lord an offering of the grain that he had grown, and Abel brought

from his flock some of the young lambs for sacrifice. There on an altar of stones they had set up in the field were their offerings. Did God accept Abel's offering and despise the other? That is the way it seemed to Cain, and he was very angry. "His countenance fell"; which means that the lines of his face were drawn down in a scowl of hatred for the brother who might be more favored than he.

"Let's go out in the field," said Cain to Abel. Then when he looked about and saw no one near, Cain struck Abel a blow so savage that Abel fell down dead.

But though Cain had not thought so, there was someone near. To Cain's guilty conscience came the voice of God: "Where is Abel, your brother?"

"I do not know," he lied, and then defiantly he asked, "Am I my brother's keeper?"

"What have you done?" came the question of God again. "The voice of your brother's blood is crying to me from the ground. And now you are cursed from the ground which has opened its mouth to receive your brother's blood. You shall be a fugitive and wanderer on the earth."

So one son of Adam and Eve was dead, and the other was a criminal. But a third was born, whose name was Seth. And Cain the fugitive, somehow and somewhere, in a way the old traditions do not explain, found himself a wife, and the human race went on. The people of Israel would claim their descent not from Cain but from Seth and from the best of his descendants, Enoch, "a man who walked with God."

But it was believed that a time came when wickedness had again got the better of what goodness there was among men, and God had to start again. In various countries of the ancient world, and especially in the great Mesopotamian plain, there were traditions of an enormous flood; the story of the flood was made by the writers of Israel into another illustration of the ways of God to choose a people fit to carry out his purposes.

> The Lord saw that the wickedness of man was great in
> the earth, and that every imagination of the thoughts of

his heart was only evil continually. And the Lord was sorry that he had made man on the earth, and it grieved him to his heart. So the Lord said, "I will blot out man whom I have created from the face of the ground, man and beast and creeping things and birds of the air, for I am sorry that I have made them.

But there was one righteous man, whose name was Noah. He and all his family had been behaving themselves. So it seemed that the best thing to do would be to separate Noah and his household from the rest of the human population, and see whether the world could be reformed.

The Lord told Noah, "The end of all flesh is come." The wicked people had been wicked long enough. There would be a flood such as there had never been since the world began, and nearly everybody would perish in it. Everybody except Noah and his family.

Meanwhile, Noah was to build a boat—not just an ordinary boat—but a great thing like a floating house, to be called the ark, three stories high, with doors and windows. It would have to be big, because Noah was to take into it not only his family but a male and female of all the living creatures on the earth.

So Noah went to work, according to the directions the Lord had given him. The story as it is written in the Book of Genesis does not stop to describe the scene, but it is easy to think how it must have been imagined by the people who listened to it as it was handed down from generation to generation. Here was a man building a great boat on dry land. And what for? Where was any water to float it in? Noah must have lost his wits. That is what all the neighbors could have been saying as they stood around and laughed.

But the day came when it was no laughing matter. It began to rain. Down the rain fell, harder and harder. Forty days and forty nights it rained, while the flood waters spread through the plains and covered the hills, and drowned every living thing that had been left on the earth.

Only Noah and his family and the animals he had taken with him were left alive in the ark.

At last the rain stopped and the flood subsided. Then one day there was a scraping sound and the bottom of the ark touched something solid. It was the top of Mount Ararat; but over the rest of the earth the waters still prevailed.

Noah opened one of the windows of the ark and let loose a dove. But the dove came back again, because there was nowhere any solid ground yet on which she could alight.

After seven days, Noah sent out the dove again, and this time she came back with an olive leaf in her bill. So Noah knew that the flood was receding. The next time Noah sent out the dove, she did not return. It meant that the flood was over. Then, at long last, Noah could open the doors of the ark, and he and his family and the animals came out. And the beautiful tradition written into the narrative was that God gave Noah then the sign of a new covenant; that there would be no such flood again, and that "while the earth remaineth, seed time and harvest, and cold and heat, and summer and winter, and day and night, shall not cease." And the sign of this promise was the rainbow which, when the rain clouds of the flood broke up and the sun came out, shone for the first time in the sky.

With all the people except Noah's family drowned, it might have been supposed that the earth was washed clear of all its wickedness forever, but the scribes to whom we owe the Book of Genesis knew that life did not work out that way. So, at the end of the story of the flood, there comes an unhappy sequence. When Noah got out of the ark and onto the good earth again, he planted a vineyard; and when the grapes were ripe and made into wine, Noah got drunk. Not only that, but one of his sons treated him indecently. And the tradition as written into the Book of Genesis made that son the ancestor of the nations which the people of Israel afterwards came to hate: the hostile tribes of Canaan, and the Assyrians and the Babylonians. It would be a satisfaction to be able to think that those peoples belonged to the wicked who deserved to be under a curse.

Another very old tradition is preserved in the eleventh chapter of the Book of Genesis. It is the story of the Tower of Babel. In ancient Babylon there were the ziggurats, great temple structures raised tier after tier above the plain to the altars at the top. It was as though the power and pride of Babylon presumed to reach the sky itself and be as great as God. But "the Lord came down to see the city and the tower which the children of men builded." He confounded the speech of the builders—from which comes our word Babel. And the story of the tower which God thus prevented from being finished became at once a legend which explained how it happened that there are different languages, and also a parable of how the pride of Babylon would be brought low.

CHAPTER FIVE

Abraham Follows
the Voice of God

M OST OF the story of the people of Israel, as the Old Testament recounts it, moves among the scenes and landmarks of a clear and particular strip of the earth—the little country at the eastern border of the Mediterranean Sea that is known as Palestine. But in the early chapters of the Book of Genesis the background is wider and more dim. Where was the Garden of Eden imagined to be? And where, according to the far-off tradition, was the flood? Seemingly in that great country "between the rivers," the Tigris and the Euphrates, in the land of ancient Babylonia.

How, then, does the scene shift to Palestine, and how does the history of Israel begin to come out of the pre-dawn dimness into the light? The answer comes with the name that appears for the first time at the end of the eleventh chapter of the Book of Genesis, and with an event which showed that the great influences that remake the world may be very different from the things that were supposed to be important.

In what was once the rich and fertile valley where the waters of the Tigris and Euphrates ran, in Mesopotamia, great empires flourished. The mighty city of Babylon was built there, with lofty walls surrounding it, with towers and temples and hanging gardens that were among the wonders of the world. Three thousand years ago the power of Babylon ruled that region of the earth, and no one would have supposed that Babylon would ever fall. Later, another empire succeeded it—Assyria, with its capital at

16

Nineveh. The armies of Assyria were more terrible than those of Babylon had been; and huge stone sculptures still remain to show the bearded warriors and the horses and chariots that went on their conquering way. Here it seemed were greatness and glory that nothing could destroy. But Babylon and Nineveh now are only mounded ruins, buried deep—and for centuries forgotten—under the dust that drifted in from the empty deserts of what had once been the fertile lands.

But out of that same Mesopotamian country there came a little group of people who would mean more to history than all the crowds that walked the long-since-vanished streets of Nineveh and Babylon. In the eleventh and twelfth chapters of the Book of Genesis, the first book of the Old Testament, is the story of who they were.

In "Ur of the Chaldeans," according to that ancient record, lived a man named Terah, descended from Shem, the eldest son of Noah. The name of Terah's son was Abram. The city of Ur was situated on the Euphrates River, in the great plain south of Babylon. Like most of the other cities of its far-off time, it crumbled at length into nothingness, and even the knowledge of where it once had been was lost. But now the site of it has been re-discovered. Layers of the earth that covered it have been dug away, and enough has been found among its broken walls to show that Ur was a center of prosperous life. It was a shrine of special worship also, for in it was a great temple to the Moon-goddess, Sin.

Terah, and his son Abram, and their kinsfolk decided to leave Ur. The brief statement in the eleventh chapter of Genesis does not tell why they left, except to show where they were going.

> Terah took Abram his son and Lot the son of Haran, his grandson, and Sarai his daughter-in-law, his son Abram's wife, and they went forth together from Ur of the Chaldeans to go into the land of Canaan.

They went as far as Haran, far to the northwest of Babylon and to the west of Nineveh and were on the way to Canaan, which was the name then of what now is Palestine. It may be that Terah had

had enough of journeying by the time they reached that far, for "when they came to Haran, they settled there, and Terah died in Haran."

But something greater was to be true of Terah's son. This is the way the twelfth chapter of the Book of Genesis begins:

> Now the Lord said to Abram "Go from your country and your kindred and your father's house to the land that I will show you. And I will make of you a great nation, and I will bless you and make your name great, so that you will be a blessing . . ." So Abram went, as the Lord had told him.

On then toward the west, beyond the borders of countries he had never known before, went Abram. It was a long journey, part of it over what seemed the trackless desert sands. In many generations there have been the pioneers—men who struck out in new paths on new adventures. There is always something noble in the boldness of spirit which dares what the common crowd will not attempt. But in the going-out of Abram there was something that lifted it above the level of most events—even the great events —of history. For, in the light of the results that followed, it was seen that what stirred him was more than a human impulse—not

restless ambition, not curiosity, not any calculation of his own. Rather, it was the moving of God, which sometimes lays hold of a life and carries it on to ends greater than the man himself could dream. So it is written, later in the Bible, that Abram "went out, not knowing where he was to go." But all the while God knew, and the greatness of Abram was that he had faith enough to listen and obey.

Abram—that was his name when he started from Ur of the Chaldeans. But his name was changed to Abraham, which means "father of a multitude." In the tradition of Israel he was the great forefather of a nation. Because of him and of God's purpose as expressed in him, Israel could believe itself to be "The Chosen People"; and all the history of what was to happen in "The Holy Land" would be part of a heavenly plan.

So it is recorded in the Book of Genesis that God said to Abraham, "I will establish my covenant between me and you and your descendants after you throughout their generations for an everlasting covenant, to be God to you and to your descendants after you. And I will give to you, and to your descendants after you, the land of your sojournings, all the land of Canaan, for an everlasting possession; and I will be their God." Part of the prom-

ise was that "kings shall come forth from you"; and kings did arise among Abraham's descendants. But it was not earthly kings or kingdoms that would distinguish Abraham's people from the other nations of their world. Rather it was their faith that there is a heavenly power that judges and rules over all earthly kingdoms; and, like Abraham, they "looked for a city which has foundations, whose builder and maker is God."

The "city" at first was only a figure of speech. In time there would develop among the descendants of Abraham a gathered life and culture that would center in the Holy City of Jerusalem. But with Abraham it was a different story. With his camels and his flocks and herds, he moved here and there in the sparsely settled country, looking for springs of water or the shelter of occasional trees. And at Mamre and at Bethel, and at other places where he pitched his tents, he built his altars from stones of the fields, and worshipped God.

CHAPTER SIX

The Destruction of Sodom and Gomorrah

L OT, his nephew, had come with Abraham, and the figure of Abraham, as the great tradition was to represent it, stands out most vividly in contrast with this same Lot.

Lot had his own flocks and herds and his men who took care of them. They began to quarrel with Abraham's men. That did not seem to disturb Lot, but it did trouble Abraham.

He said to Lot, "Let there be no strife between you and me, and between your herdsmen and my herdsmen; for we are kinsmen. Is not the whole land before you? Separate yourself from me. If you take the left hand, then I will go to the right; or if you take the right hand, then I will go to the left."

Lot could have his own first choice of the pasturage that looked best; and this suited Lot exactly. He looked down from the hills of Canaan, with their rocks and their arid slopes, and he saw the valley of the Jordan River, soft and green. If Abraham was simple enough to let him have it, all well and good. He would choose that; and he did.

He did not stop to ask what else might be in that inviting valley. Sodom and Gomorrah were there, two of the wickedest cities on the earth. Anyone moving into their neighborhood might have to pay a heavy price for what he thought was his smart advantage. This was what Lot would presently find out.

After Lot had gone, Abraham was sitting one day at the entrance to his tent, which he had pitched on the plain of Mamre. He looked up and saw three men approaching. With the hospitality that has always been the mark of the desert dwellers to

21

strangers who might appear from the empty spaces, Abraham went out to welcome them. He brought them into the tent, and had water brought to wash the dust from their feet, and a meal made ready from the best food that could be found.

When the meal was finished, the men rose up to go, and Abraham walked with them part of their way. They were looking down toward Sodom and Gomorrah; and the way they looked and the questions they asked began to trouble Abraham. Who were these strangers who had not told their names? Were they men, or were they messengers from God? And what were they going down to Sodom and Gomorrah for? Could it be that they were going there to bring God's judgment on the wickedness they would surely see?

So Abraham began to pray. He knew how evil the cities were, but all the same it was awful to think that they might be utterly destroyed. Suppose there were some good people living there among the bad?

Abraham cried out to God, "Wilt thou indeed destroy the wicked?" And in the earnestness of his plea, he dared go on, "Far be it from thee to do such a thing, to slay the righteous with the wicked. Shall not the Judge of all the earth do right?"

Then in his heart he heard what he was sure was God's answer. If there were as many as fifty righteous people in Sodom, God would spare the city from destruction.

"Behold," said Abraham, "I have taken upon myself to speak to the Lord, I who am but dust and ashes. Suppose five of the fifty righteous are lacking? Wilt thou destroy the whole city for lack of five?"

No, the Lord would have pity upon Sodom for the sake of forty-five.

Still Abraham's compassionate concern drove him on to intercede.

Would God withhold his judgment from the city if there were forty righteous people in it? Or if there were thirty? Or even if there were twenty? And God answered, "For the sake of twenty, I will not destroy it."

"Oh let not the Lord be angry, and I will speak but this once," Abraham cried. "Suppose ten are found there." And for the sake of only ten, God said he would stay his hand.

But would there be ten?

That evening in the streets of Sodom appeared two men—were they two of the men who had been in Abraham's tent?—and Lot saw them. He urged them to come into his house, and finally persuaded them. But some of the vicious crowd of the city had also seen them; and they came beating on Lot's door and demanding that the men be turned over to them. But they could not get in.

Then the men—or, as the story in Genesis also calls them, the two angels—warned Lot that the end had come, and that in the morning Sodom would be destroyed. Not even ten righteous people could be counted in it. But there would be time in the first hours of dawn for Lot and his family to escape.

Nevertheless, Lot's sons-in-law laughed when he told them what was about to happen to the city. And it took the help of the two angels to get Lot and his wife and his daughters onto the road in flight. But not even all of those were saved. In the region round the Dead Sea where Sodom and Gomorrah are supposed to have stood, there are places where oil and pitch bubble up from the ground. The "fire and brimstone rained from heaven" may have been a lightning bolt that made the oil burst into flames, while a furious wind blew the conflagration upon the cities. It was a time for desperate haste. But Lot's wife still wanted to be in Sodom. She stopped to look back; and the wind and the fire and the fumes from the Dead Sea overwhelmed her, so that a continuing tradition among the Bedouins points to the place where Lot's wife "was turned into a pillar of salt."

CHAPTER SEVEN

Abraham and Sarah and Isaac

M EANWHILE, what of Abraham? Up to this point he has been the man who followed what would seem in any age to be the right thought and the right choice. But now comes an account that must be considered not according to the standards of the 20th century A.D., but in the light of what was familiar and everywhere accepted among the peoples of the ancient east. As an ideal at least, monogamy belongs in the code of required morals. But in the time of Abraham there was no thought of anything discreditable in a man's having more than one wife.

Abraham's wife was Sarah, and Sarah was growing old. The great sorrow of both of them was that they had no child. So Sarah let Abraham take her maid, Hagar, and treat her as though she were his wife.

But when presently Hagar had a child, Sarah was jealous. The servant girl had given Abraham the son and heir that she, Sarah, had not been able to give. She could not bear the sight of Hagar any more. So she drove Hagar out of the tents into the desert.

In the Book of Genesis there are two stories of Sarah driving Hagar out, which is one of the illustrations of the fact already mentioned that various traditions as they came down from the ancient time—even when they differed—were put together in the Book. But in both the stories the name of Hagar's son is Ishmael, and in both an angel of the Lord finds Hagar as she wanders in despair and saves her. Ishmael, the son of Abraham and Hagar, would be "a wild man, his hand against every man, and every

24

man's hand against him," and he would be the ancestor of the Arab tribes who thus would be blood kin to all the other descendants of Abraham, but of an illegitimate line.

But how could there be other descendants of Abraham when the very reason for the birth of Ishmael was that Sarah, Abraham's wife, was old, and could never now have a child of her own?

Here again appears the golden thread of proud belief that runs through all the Old Testament story of those who believed themselves to be "the Chosen People." As God had called Abraham from Ur of the Chaldees to create a new nation, so God himself would see that the promise was fulfilled. Therefore Sarah did conceive and bear a son, when it had seemed that this would be impossible. The name given to him was Isaac, which means *he laughs;* and there was great rejoicing at his birth.

But then follows the scene which might have ended in horror, the meaning of which grows clear only when one remembers the dark beliefs from which in the world of Abraham's time men were not yet delivered. Among early peoples the gods could be thought of as cruel and implacable in their demanding. Nothing

that the worshiper had might be too much for the gods to insist
upon and take. So the conception of what was sufficient worship
moved on to its fearful climax—to human sacrifice. To offer the
fruits of the earth, or a lamb from the flock, might not be enough.
A man's own child, "the fruit of thy body," might have to be offered up before the gods were satisfied.

That is what some of the peoples in the region of Canaan believed. It may have been that Abraham looked at them, and asked
himself the awful question—if they were moved to that extreme
obedience to their gods, ought he to stop at less in the name of
the God who had led him out of Ur? Must he offer Isaac?

So the voice within his conscience seemed to say, "Take your
son, your only son Isaac whom you love, and go to the land of
Moriah, and offer him there as a burnt offering upon one of the
mountains of which I shall tell you."

Early in the morning Abraham rose (was Sarah sleeping so that
she could not know?). He had his ass saddled, and he took two of
his servants, and wood to kindle the fire of sacrifice, and Isaac.

A three days' journey they went, until he came to the place of
which he had had his dreadful indication. "Stay here with the
ass," he said to the servants. "I and the lad will go yonder and
worship, and come again to you." He did not tell them what the
worship was to be; nor could he bear to let them know that when
he came back, he would come alone.

So he and Isaac "went both of them together." He laid the
wood on Isaac's shoulder; and in his own hands he had a brand of
fire, and a knife.

"My father," said Isaac.

And Abraham answered, "Here am I, my son."

"Here are the fire and the wood," said Isaac; "but where is the
lamb for a burnt offering?"

And all that the agonized Abraham could answer was, "God
will provide himself a lamb for a burnt offering, my son."

Abraham built an altar, laid the wood upon it, bound Isaac,
and laid him on the altar too. The knife was in his hand.

Then, at that instant, there came to Abraham an angel's voice, "Do not lay your hand on the lad or do anything to him, for now I know that you fear God, seeing you have not withheld your son, your only son."

The great lesson had been learned. The God who was guiding the steps of Abraham was not like the deities of the groping peoples round about. Among the descendants of Abraham human sacrifice would never be performed. They were to learn, as one of the prophets was afterwards to proclaim, that "to do justly and to love mercy" is "to walk humbly with thy God."

The journey, which Abraham had begun with such a heavy heart, ended now in thankfulness and joy. Isaac was to live, and to fulfil the purpose of the Lord.

CHAPTER EIGHT

Rebekah Comes
as Isaac's Bride

THE YEARS went by, and it was time for Isaac to be married. But not to any girl who had grown up in one of the families of Canaan, Abraham thought. A bride for Isaac ought to come from among his kindred and so be of his own kind.

So Abraham called his trusted servant, Eliezer. "Swear by the Lord," he said, "the God of heaven and of the earth, that you will not take a wife for my son from the daughters of the Canaanites, among whom I dwell, but will go to my country and to my kindred, and take a wife for my son Isaac."

So Eliezer took ten of Abraham's camels, and ladened some of them with gifts; and he and other servants in his charge set out along the roads by which Abraham himself had come when he first set out for Canaan. To the north and then to the east the caravan rocked on its way, beneath the gleaming snowy peak of Mount Hermon, past the gardens of Damascus, through the heavy sands of long desert miles, until it came at length to the country which once had been Abraham's home. And there, in Mesopotamia at last, near a village called Nahor, Eliezer halted the caravan by a well.

It was evening, and the women and girls of the village would be coming out to draw water. This was the country of Abraham's kindred, and somewhere there might be the girl that Eliezer had come to find and bring home as Isaac's bride. But how should he know her if she should appear?

Eliezer prayed, "O Lord, God of my master Abraham, grant me success today!" He pleaded that something might happen that would make the one girl he was looking for seem different from all the others.

Before his prayer was finished, he saw the women of the village coming. Among them, with a water jar upon her shoulder, was a maiden, very fair to look upon. She went down to the spring, and filled her jar and came up.

Eliezer went toward her.

"Will you give me a little water to drink," he asked.

"Drink, my lord," she said; and she gave him the jar, to drink from it as he might desire.

But that was not all. She looked at the caravan, with the tired camels kneeling at the borders of the well. "I will draw for your camels also," she said, "as much as they can drink." And back to the spring she went, and filled her jar again and again, until even the thirsty camels had had enough.

Now Eliezer's heart rejoiced. He had had his sign as to the sort of girl she was.

"Tell me whose daughter you are," he said. And would there be room in her father's house for him to lodge that night?

She told him her name. She was Rebekah, the daughter of Bethuel. And as to her father's house, she held out welcome with the same quick gladness with which she had given him the water at the well. "We have both straw and provender enough, and room to lodge in," she said to Eliezer. And Eliezer bowed his head and offered his thanksgiving, "Blessed be the Lord, the God of my master Abraham, who has not forgotten his steadfast love and faithfulness toward my master. As for me, the Lord has led me in the way." And from the pack on one of the camels he took a gold ring and two bracelets, and he put them on Rebekah's finger and on her arms.

By this time Laban, Rebekah's brother, had seen the caravan; and, coming out to meet Eliezer, he had invited him into his father's house. He helped unload the camels, he brought water for the men to wash their dusty feet, and he set food before Eliezer. But Eliezer said, "I will not eat until I have told my errand."

Then he recited all the story of his coming: the charge that Abraham had given him to find a bride for Isaac; his prayer that

God would guide him; and the answer to his prayers in Rebekah at the well.

Now would they let Rebekah go home with him?

Bethuel, Rebekah's father, and Laban her brother answered, "This comes from the Lord. Let her be the wife of your master's son, as the Lord has spoken."

Then Eliezer brought out more presents for Rebekah, and costly ornaments also for her mother and her brother; and he and his men slept that night in Bethuel's house.

In the morning Eliezer was eager to start on his homeward way. Rebekah's family begged him to tarry longer, but he was urgent. Then they called Rebekah and asked her, "Will you go with this man?" And she answered, "I will go."

Back toward Canaan therefore Eliezer turned the camels' steps; and at length the caravan drew near to where the tents of Abraham would be. In the narrative of Genesis there is a sentence so beautiful that its very syllables make music. "Isaac went out to meditate in the field at the eventide, and he lifted up his eyes, and saw, and, behold, the camels were coming."

So Eliezer's mission had succeeded. He had brought Rebekah home to Isaac, and she became his wife.

CHAPTER NINE

Jacob Outwits
His Brother Esau

THUS ABRAHAM could rejoice that his hope for Isaac had been fulfilled. But sorrow also had come to him; and it is part of the richness of the Book of Genesis that the varied events and emotions which make up the mystery of human life are all reflected in it—death as well as birth, grief as well as gladness, the ends as well as the beginnings.

Sarah had died; and where should she be buried? Although Abraham had come into Canaan at the command of the Lord, there was still a sense in which this country where he had pitched his tents was foreign land. No graves of his kindred were there, no natural place of his own in which to bury Sarah. So he had to go to the Hittite people near him and say, "I am a stranger and a sojourner among you; give me property among you for a burying place, that I may bury my dead." They sold him a cave at Machpelah; and there in the cave, which the Moslems who now control the region guard as a holy place, according to the age-old tradition Sarah was buried. And there later, when Abraham died, he was buried too.

In the narrative of Genesis thus far, as in the prayers of Eliezer, the Lord is spoken of as "the God of Abraham." Later he would be called "the God of Abraham, Isaac and Jacob." So the story goes on to show the further unfolding purpose of God as this would be revealed in the life of Isaac and the life of Isaac's son.

Isaac and Rebekah had two sons, but one of them rather than the other would become the great figure in the history of those whose faith in the Lord made them the Chosen People. The two sons were twins; and the first to be born was Esau. The younger twin was Jacob.

Although they were twins, there was little likeness between them. Esau grew up to be an out-of-doors man, strong and hearty, liking best of all to hunt. He would go out and kill a deer, and bring in the fresh meat, especially for his father. Isaac was growing old; he could not do what this big son of his could do, and he depended on him more and more. When the time came for Isaac to give his final blessing, it was Esau who would have it.

Jacob was of a different sort. He did not like to roam the fields and woods as Esau did. He was more apt to be found where his mother was, helping about the tents. And he was his mother's favorite. Rebekah, who as a girl had showed by the well that she could be so complete in kindness, now as a woman showed that she could have a devotion equally complete—but also passionate and partial. Jacob meant more to her than Esau, and Isaac was not going to put Esau first in everything if she could help it.

Leaving out Isaac and Rebekah, probably anyone who saw the two brothers for the first time would have liked Esau best. He was the warm-blooded and the warm-hearted one, generous and impulsive, never stopping to bother about what he thought were little things. Jacob was quieter, and thought more—and it was not easy to know what he was thinking. With Esau it was plain enough. What interested him at any moment was written all over him, for it had to do with what he was feeling there and then. If he wanted to hunt, he would go and hunt. If he came back hungry, he would have what he wanted to eat. His thought was to get first the satisfaction that came hour by hour, and never mind what might happen after that.

Now Esau, as the eldest son, would be the inheritor of "the birthright." That meant that his father would give him his utmost blessing and he would be the head of the family: not only to be the one whose word would count most in family affairs, but also to be the one who would speak for the family to God. He would be the heir of the covenant which God had made with Abraham and his descendants.

All that might be very well; but when the impulses and appetites of his body were at their peak, Esau could forget what mattered most.

One day he had been out for a long, hard hunt. In the evening he came back toward the tents, tired and famished, with his big frame crying out for food to eat. He smelled something cooking. Then he saw Jacob bending over a pot upon the fire, and it seemed to Esau that that hot food was what he wanted more than anything else on earth. "Feed me with that pottage," he said to Jacob. "Give me some before I faint!"

This was the sort of moment that Jacob had been waiting for. "Will you sell me your birthright if I give you this," he asked of Esau.

"I am nearly dead," Esau blurted out. "What good is the birthright to anybody as hungry as I am?" Yes, he would trade the birthright for Jacob's pottage. And he did. So, as the Book of Genesis puts it, "Esau despised his birthright"; and later in the Bible he is put down as the man who was "profane," in the great, but almost forgotten, meaning of that word as one who is contemptuous of sacred things.

But, though Esau had thus traded off the birthright to Jacob, there was still the question for Jacob as to how he could actually get it. It had to come through his father's blessing. And how could he manage to have that blessing given him when he knew as well as anyone that Isaac loved Esau best?

If Jacob did not have the answer, Rebekah did. A day came when Esau had gone out hunting again. Isaac had said to him, "I am old; I do not know the day of my death. Now then, take your bow, and go out to the field and hunt game for me; and prepare savory food, such as I love, and bring it to me that I may eat; that I may bless you before I die."

Rebekah called Jacob. She told him to go and select two kids from the flock, and she would make a dish from them that Jacob should carry in to Isaac before Esau could come back with his venison; and Isaac should bless Jacob instead of Esau.

But how could Jacob pretend to be Esau so that Isaac would think he *was* Esau?

Rebekah had an answer to that too. Isaac was growing blind, so that by sight he could not tell one of his sons from the other. Suppose, though, he laid his hands on Jacob and knew the difference that way; for the big, virile Esau was a hairy man, while Jacob's skin was smooth. Then *this* was the thing to do, Rebekah decided. She made Jacob put on some of Esau's clothes, and she took some of the skin of the kids and fastened it on the back of Jacob's hands and on his neck. And she gave him the meat she had prepared and told him to take it in to Isaac.

So Jacob went into the tent where Isaac was.

"Father," he said.

"Here I am," Isaac answered. "Who are you, my son?" And Jacob said, "I am Esau your first-born; now sit up and eat of my game, that you may bless me."

"How is it that you have found it so quickly, my son?" the old man asked; and Jacob was driven to a worse lie than the one he

had spoken before. "Because the Lord has granted me success," he said.

Still Isaac was troubled. "Come near that I may feel you," he said, "that I may know whether you are really my son Esau or not." And as Jacob knelt before him and Isaac touched the skin of the kids which Rebekah had fastened on the back of Jacob's hands, he said, "The voice is Jacob's voice, but the hands are the hands of Esau."

So he took from Jacob the meat which Jacob had brought; and after he had eaten, he said, "Come near and kiss me, my son." Then as he touched Esau's clothes which Jacob had put on, the clothes that smelled of the field and the woods, he thought surely that this was Esau, and he gave Jacob the birthright blessing.

> May God give you of the dew of heaven
> and of the fatness of the earth,
> and plenty of grain and wine.
> Let peoples serve you,
> and nations bow down to you.
> Be lord over your brothers
> and may your mother's sons bow down to you.

Hardly had Jacob gone out when Esau came in from his hunting. He cooked the venison and brought it to his father.

"Who are you?" asked Isaac.

"I am your son, your first-born, Esau," he said.

Then Isaac trembled violently, and he stammered, "Who was it then that hunted game and brought it to me, and I ate it all before you came, and I have blessed him?"

Then Esau realized that he had been defrauded, and he gave a great and exceeding bitter cry. "Bless me, even me also, O my father! Have you not reserved a blessing for me?"

So Isaac gave him all the blessing that his love could express. But he could not take back the blessing of the birthright which he had already given Jacob, and which Esau had sold for "the mess of pottage."

CHAPTER TEN

Jacob's Flight, and His Return

HOT ANGER burned in Esau. Jacob had defrauded him, and he would settle accounts with Jacob—but not yet. Isaac, the old father whom he loved, seemed so feeble that he might be near his death, and Esau did not want him to be distressed. But when Isaac should be no longer alive, and the days of mourning had been observed, then he would kill Jacob.

Rebekah watched Esau, and she could tell what was in Esau's mind. She told Jacob that the thing for him to do was to get away, as fast and far as he could go. But she tried not to let it seem that she was afraid of Esau. She pretended to Isaac that the reason Jacob ought to leave home was to find a wife. As for the girls anywhere around, Rebekah said she had no use for them. Jacob ought to go and look for a bride in the country from which his mother had come.

So Jacob was sent away, on a long and lonely journey.

The country through which he went at first was desolate and barren. When night came there was no place to lie down except upon a rocky hillside, and if he wanted anything to put under his head, there was nothing but a stone.

He was so tired, though, that he went to sleep; and in his sleep he had a dream. In that dream he saw a ladder set up on the earth, with the top of it reaching to the sky; and the angels of God were going up the ladder and also coming down. And he seemed to hear the voice of God promising him that God would go with him, and some day bring him home again. And when he woke from his dream and looked out again at the country around him, still so stark and bleak, he said, "Surely the Lord was in this place, even when I did not know it." So he made an altar of the stones, and he called the place Bethel, which means the House of God.

But why should such a dream—a dream of angels on a ladder between the earth and heaven—have come to a man like Jacob? This man who had wronged his brother—what did he have to do with God? If either brother was ever to be used for God's purposes, why should it not have been Esau—and not Jacob?

The reason would appear only in the years to follow. There were many lessons for Jacob to learn and hard discipline to be endured. But there was one difference between him and Esau which showed why he in the end, in spite of his mean beginning, might become the greater man. He was reaching after something higher than Esau was concerned with. He wanted the birthright because the birthright meant being the representative of the family in trying to keep the covenant with God. Esau lived mostly according to the impulses of his body. Jacob, unworthy as he was, at least remembered that he had a soul.

From Bethel he went on his way, heading eastward all the time. He was trying to reach his mother's country, and the village where her brother, Laban, lived.

At length he did arrive. There at the end of the path he saw a well—the very well by which Eliezer, the messenger, first had seen Rebekah as a girl. And now there happened almost exactly what had happened in the same place years before. This time there was another girl coming out at evening to draw water for her sheep. As soon as Jacob saw her, he fell in love with her, for she was young and beautiful. And when she had asked him his name and learned who his mother was, she ran and told her father—who was Laban, Rebekah's brother.

Laban welcomed Jacob, and he told Jacob that he could live there and work for wages. But there was one thing above everything that Jacob now was bent upon. He wanted to marry Rachel. He would work for Laban seven years if he might have her for his wife.

So he did work seven years, and then at last he could be married. According to the eastern custom, the bride was veiled, so that not

until the marriage was finished should the bridegroom see her face. Then as Jacob held her hand, the veil was lifted—and it was not Rachel. It was her older sister, Leah!

Jacob, who had deceived Esau, had been himself deceived. Laban said that according to the custom of the country, the older sister ought to be married first, and so Jacob had to have Leah instead of Rachel.

But it was Rachel that Jacob loved, and he said he would work for Laban seven more years if at the end of that time he might have Rachel. And he did.

Now Jacob had had enough of Laban. He decided that he would go back again to Canaan, where he had been born and where he had lived until he had fled from what he thought was Esau's deadly anger. So he told Leah and Rachel that he was going. He gathered together all the flocks and herds that belonged to him—for he had been smarter than Laban; and he put Rachel and Leah and the children who had been born to him on his camels, and he set out before Laban knew that he had gone. For seven days Laban pursued him and caught up with Jacob's caravan at length. Though at first he tried to compel Jacob to come back he could not do so, and finally they parted in peace.

The garden in Eden which God made for Adam and Eve.

"And the flood was forty days upon the earth, and all the high hills were covered."

Lot and his family flee from burning Sodom.

Rebekah is brought to be the bride of Isaac.

But what would lie ahead for Jacob? The country to which he was returning was Esau's country, and who could know whether or not Esau's old impulse to kill Jacob might break out now into a flame of murderous vengeance if he knew that Jacob was daring to come home?

The worst thing to do—it seemed to Jacob—would be to risk coming upon Esau suddenly. The best thing would be to send messengers who would speak for him to his brother. So some of Jacob's servants were dispatched ahead, with instructions to say to Esau that Jacob, their master, begged Esau to let him come.

But the servants came back late in the day with terrifying tidings. They had not got to Esau, for Esau himself was advancing, and with him four hundred men.

Jacob was more afraid than ever, but he thought quickly. No matter what it cost, he must try to soften Esau's mood. He divided all his flocks and herds into three, and he ordered his servants to drive them toward Esau, the first group well ahead of the others, and the second ahead of the third. When the first met Esau, they were to say that everything they were bringing was a present from Jacob; and when the second and the third came they were to say the same. Meanwhile Jacob and his family would still be behind; and they would come into Esau's presence only after Esau had been enriched by nearly everything that Jacob had.

That seemed to Jacob his best hope. Now there was nothing to do, for the day had gone and the servants with the flocks could not start out until the morning.

That night something happened which was to change the rest of Jacob's life. The account of it in the Book of Genesis is a mingling of different interpretations, coming down the stream of far-off tradition like cloudy waters merging with the clear. Among the superstitions of the early peoples was the belief that particular places belonged to particular spirits, invisible but real and dangerous. In the day time they might have no power; but in the dark they were always there.

Thinking of Esau and of what might happen the next morning, Jacob could not sleep. He went out and walked by a brook that ran near where he had camped. He was alone—alone in the black night. Then, out of the shadows came a dreadful something—something that "wrestled with him until the breaking of the day." The first tellers of the story may have thought of this as the river-god, disputing the passage of the river; a river-god that said to Jacob at length "Let me go for the day is breaking," since such a spirit had power only in the dark. But there was the deeper meaning for those who could understand. What Jacob wrestled with was no river-god. It was the awful power of a guilty conscience sent to seize him and make him settle his accounts with God. And the thing that could make Jacob into a man at last was that he did not evade the struggle. He would try to make what had happened end in good. All through the night he wrestled, and to the terrible force that held him he said at last, "I will not let you go, unless you bless me.".

At the end of the struggle Jacob's thigh was out of joint, and from that time on he would be lame. He would carry scars forever. But in what would become the undying faith of the Chosen People, he would be the symbol of a desire for God that they never would let go. And so the story of the wrestling at the river Jabbok ends with the words of the dark antagonist who could also be God's messenger: "Your name shall no more be called Jacob, but Israel, for you have striven with God and with men, and have prevailed."

No wonder that at the end of the narrative it is written that Jacob called the name of the place Penuel, which means *the face of God;* and that as he passed over the river, "the sun rose upon him."

Esau was coming that day; but it would all prove to be completely different from what Jacob had feared. Esau, the hot-blooded, was also the great-hearted. He was big enough to be able to forgive. So when Jacob first caught sight of him and bowed himself seven times to the ground, Esau ran and embraced him and kissed him, and they both wept.

"What did you mean by all these companies that I have met?" asked Esau; and Jacob answered, "To find favor in the sight of my Lord."

But Esau said, "I have enough, my brother; keep what you have for yourself."

"Let us journey on our way, and I will go before you," said Esau. But Jacob replied that the children were weary, and the flocks were tired too; so Esau might go on, and he would follow slowly.

Then he went on toward a village called Shechem, where he bought some land to pitch his tents; but soon after that he went on to Bethel, and built an altar there—the Bethel which was the place where long years before he had seen his vision of the ladder set up from earth to heaven, and the angels of God ascending and descending it.

CHAPTER ELEVEN

The Boy with
the Brilliant Dreams

THE FAULTS that had been in Jacob were plain enough, but always there had been something in him besides his faults. He was a man who could hold on, in spite of failures and humiliations. And he was capable of deep devotion.

From the first moment he saw her he had loved Rachel, and that love for her never changed. In the same way he loved especially Rachel's sons. When Benjamin, the second of them, was born Rachel had died; and now Joseph, her first-born, and Benjamin were the center of Jacob's life, as their mother had been before. Because he had been married first to Leah, and had treated two servant girls as though they were his wives, he had other sons; but some of them were to bring him mostly trouble.

These older sons of Jacob—and there were ten of them—grew up into the sort of men who can settle down into a rut where they began, and stay there. They did not like anything that meant new thinking. Stay where you are, do what you have always done, let well enough alone—that was what they thought was sensible. And they did not want anyone to tell them something else.

But Joseph was different. He had imagination. He was sure that life was meant to be big and wonderful. He kept having dreams about what might happen to him; and he was innocent enough to think that his brothers would like to hear what he had dreamed.

He told them that one night he had a dream that they had all been gathering up the cut grain in the field and binding it in

42

sheaves, and his sheaf stood up and the sheaves of all the rest of them bowed down to his. And another night he dreamed that the sun and moon and eleven stars made obeisance to him—to Joseph.

It was natural enough that his brothers were annoyed. And they were annoyed all the more when they saw how their father favored Joseph. He had given him a special colored coat, such as none of the other brothers had.

Then the trouble was that they began to talk about it and make the whole thing much worse than it was. Instead of treating Joseph's dreams as a young boy's notions that could do no harm to them, they told each other that they all had been insulted. Joseph ought to be put in his proper place.

There came a day when the older brothers were out in the fields, and Jacob sent Joseph out to carry them a message. They looked up and saw who was approaching. "Look, here is that dreamer!" they said. Or put in rougher words, what they meant was this, "Here comes that brat with the big ideas!"

Suddenly it seemed that they had had all they could stand of Joseph. Why not get rid of him? "Let's kill him and throw his body into a pit," said one of them. But Reuben said, "No, not kill him." The better thing to do would be to sell him to someone who would carry him off as a slave.

By chance just then there came in sight a caravan of Ishmaelites from across the Jordan, their camels laden with spices which they were carrying down into Egypt. So they sold Joseph to the Ishmaelites for twenty pieces of silver; and presently the caravan, and Joseph with it, had disappeared in the distance of the dusty road.

Then they took Joseph's coat, dipped it in the blood of a kid they killed, took it back to Jacob, and told him that Joseph must have been killed by some wild beast. And Jacob rent his clothes and put on sack cloth and mourned for Joseph many days.

Meanwhile there began with Joseph the story that would be great or not, according to the way it ended. It might have ended either way.

Here was the boy who at home had been his father's favorite; and now he had no home, and no one near him cared whether he lived or died. He had had his lofty dreams of what he thought God meant for him to be, and now he was nothing but a slave. What was the use of believing in anything any more? Why not let life just go to pieces?

Even so, there was worse to come.

Joseph was sold by the Ishmaelites to Potiphar, an officer in the bodyguard of Pharaoh, King of Egypt. As time went by, Potiphar began to like him, for he saw that this slave could be trusted. At length he was so sure of Joseph that he put him in charge of all his household, and gave himself no concern about anything that Joseph did.

But Potiphar was not the only one that Joseph had to reckon with. There was Potiphar's wife. She was a passionate woman, who could be dangerous. When she saw that Joseph was young and handsome, she fell in love with him; and she tried again and again to tempt Joseph to make love to her.

Why not? Joseph might have said. After all that had happened to him, why should he have any scruples? Who could expect him to live for anything except what the moment offered?

But that was not Joseph. He had a sense of honor that stood by him, no matter what the temptation was. Potiphar had trusted him, and he was not going to betray that trust. "My master has put everything that he has in my hand," he said to her; "nor has he kept back anything from me except yourself, because you are his wife. How then can I do this great wickedness, and sin against God?"

Baffled now in her desire, the feeling that Potiphar's wife had had for Joseph turned into fury. She had tried for one last time to drag him to her, and when he tore himself away she caught hold of his robe and a piece of it ripped off in her hand. She called some of the servants and showed it to them. Joseph, she said, had been attacking her.

When Potiphar came home, she met him with the same lie. "The Hebrew servant, whom you have brought among us, came in to me to insult me," she told him. And she said that it was only when she had screamed that Joseph had fled out of the house.

Supposing that what she said was true, Potiphar acted with instant anger. There was no time for Joseph to plead his own cause; and who would have believed him if he had? He was sent off immediately to one of Pharaoh's prisons. He had been sold by his brothers into Egypt. Now—not because of any wrong that he had done but because of wrong done to him—he found himself in jail among the criminals.

But something about Joseph caught the notice of the jailer, just as it had caught the notice of Potiphar once before. Here was somebody who could bear responsibility. So the jailer made Joseph a sort of deputy, with authority over the others who were locked up in the prison.

Among those other prisoners were two who had been sent there from Pharaoh's court. One of them had been the king's butler; the other had been the baker. In the prison each of them had a dream and they told their dreams to Joseph. He listened to them, and he told them what their dreams might mean.

Dreams again—but there was a difference now. Years before, in the home land, Joseph had had his own dreams. But the trouble with those dreams was that they all had to do with himself. What would he get out of life? What advantages would come to *him?* Never mind about anybody else.

But since he had been in Egypt another side of Joseph had developed. The furnace of affliction might have destroyed him altogether. Instead, it had burned away some of the dross and brought out in his character what was good. He had learned that the world was not limited to Joseph. Other people mattered. So he could be faithful to Potiphar, whatever came. And so, even in the prison, he could forget about himself and try to help the others who were worse off than he.

CHAPTER TWELVE

The Reward of Faithfulness

N ow the great things which Joseph had believed that God intended for his life were about to come true. The dream of Pharaoh's butler which Joseph had interpreted meant, said Joseph, that the butler would be pardoned and brought back to serve at Pharaoh's table again. That was what happened. The butler had promised that he would never cease thanking Joseph and he would never forget him; but he did forget him all the same, until he heard that Pharaoh himself had had a dream which troubled him, and which he could not understand. Then the butler got word to Pharaoh about the man in his prison, and Pharaoh ordered that Joseph should be brought to him.

"I have heard it said of you," said Pharaoh, "that when you hear a dream you can interpret it."

Joseph replied that answers could not come from any wisdom of his own, but God might show him the meaning of a dream.

Then Pharaoh told of how he had dreamed twice. In one dream he said, he was standing on the banks of the Nile, and seven cows, fat and sleek, came up out of the Nile and fed in the reed grass; and seven other cows came up after them, poor and very gaunt and thin, and ate up the seven fat cows. But when they had eaten them no one would have known that they had eaten, for they were still as gaunt as at the beginning.

The second dream was much like that one, only, instead of seven cows, there were seven good ears of grain; and seven withered and blighted ears destroyed the good ones.

Joseph listened. He knew these were dreams that concerned what might be a whole people's fate.

He told Pharaoh that the seven fat cows and the seven full heads of grain meant that there would be seven years of plenty in the land of Egypt; but that there would come seven years of famine which would eat up all that the good years had produced. What Pharaoh needed to do was to get ready. In the seven good years all the extra harvests must be gathered up and stored, so that there would be something to live on when the famine came.

Pharaoh looked at Joseph. This man had made sense of his dreams. If a famine was to come, who could prepare for it so well as this one who foresaw it? He would put Joseph in power to do what needed to be done.

"All my people shall order themselves as you command," he said; "only as regards the throne will I be greater than you." He took a signet ring and put it on Joseph's finger, he arrayed him in garments of fine linen, and put a gold chain about his neck; and he ordered that one of the royal chariots should be ready to drive him where he chose to go. "Without your consent," he said, "no man shall move hand or foot in all the land of Egypt."

The man who had come into Egypt as a slave was lifted now to authority only less than Pharaoh's own.

For seven years the valley of the Nile brought forth the rich harvests which men always hoped for from the deep earth there by the life-giving river. Joseph went through all Egypt, and saw to it that the abundant grain was gathered up and carried from the fields to storehouses built in every city. There was food that seemed as limitless as the sands of the sea.

But then the change came. Something happened to the inundation of the Nile which every spring had brought fertility to the fields. The ground grew hard and dry. No seed sprouted. Everywhere people were in distress.

Joseph opened the storehouses and began to issue food. But it was not only the Egyptians who cried out for it. The famine was in other lands also. As hunger spread in the regions round about, men turned in desperation to wherever food might be.

In the years since Joseph had disappeared, Jacob, his father, had mourned for him. He had given him up for dead. When rumor reached Canaan that grain was stored in Egypt, Jacob had no idea Joseph was there and that he had anything to do with Egypt's store. But only in that direction was there any hope.

CHAPTER THIRTEEN

The Guilty Brothers
Come to Joseph

J ACOB SAID to his sons, "I have heard that there is grain in Egypt;
go down and buy it for us there, that we may live, and not
die." All the older sons were to go together; but he would not let
them take Benjamin, Joseph's one full brother, Rachel's other son.

Down into Egypt, therefore, the sons of Jacob came—the same
men who once had sold Joseph to the Ishmaelites. When they
asked where they should go to beg for food or for the chance to
buy it, they were told to go to the man whom Pharaoh had made
governor of the land.

At length they came into Joseph's presence. This royal figure
before whom they bowed down was to them as someone whom
they could not imagine ever having seen before. Joseph recog-
nized them, but he did not let them know it.

"Where do you come from?" he said.

"From the land of Canaan," they answered, "to buy food."

"You are spies," he said. "What you have come for is to see the
weakness of the land."

Frightened, they began to tell about themselves.

"No, my Lord," they said, "to buy food have we come. Your
servants are not spies. We are twelve brothers, the sons of one man
in the land of Canaan. The youngest is this day with our father,
and one is no more."

Joseph would try them out; and also what he yearned for most
was to see again his brother Benjamin.

"You are spies," he said. "This is how you shall be tested. By the life of Pharaoh, you shall not go from this place unless your youngest brother comes here. Send one of you, and let him bring your brother, while you remain in prison."

He kept them three days and then he demanded that they should bring Benjamin down to Egypt. He would take one of them, Simeon, and keep him as a hostage. He would sell food to the others to carry home. Then they were to come back, and Benjamin was to come with them.

As Joseph gave them his command, they looked at one another. Now that they were in trouble, old memories rose up to haunt them. They remembered how they had sold Joseph, and had shut their ears when he had cried out at what they meant to do. "We are guilty," they said, "because we saw his distress and would not listen. That is why this trouble now has come upon us." And they did not know that Joseph understood what they were saying.

The other brothers did leave Simeon, and set out on their way to Canaan. There was nothing else to do.

When they returned home they brought the sacks of grain which Joseph had let them have in Egypt. But before long all that food was gone and Jacob said to them that they must go again and try to buy more.

But Judah answered for all the sons. "The man solemnly warned us, 'You shall not see my face unless your brother is with you.' So if you will send Benjamin with us, we will go down and buy you food. But if you will not send him, we will not go."

Why had they ever told the man that they had another brother? Jacob asked. There was no way they could have kept it back, they answered. "The man questioned us carefully about ourselves and our kindred, saying, 'Is your father still alive? Have you another brother?' Could we know that he would say 'Bring your brother down'?"

Then Judah pleaded with his father to let Benjamin go. He would be surety for him, and stake his life to bring him back.

Mournfully Jacob gave consent. "May God Almighty grant you mercy before the man," he said, "that he may send back Simeon and Benjamin. If I am bereaved of my children, I am bereaved."

Events moved rapidly now toward their climax. This time the older brothers took Benjamin with them as they went down to Egypt. When Joseph saw him, he was so filled with emotion that he could not control himself. He went off by himself and wept. Then when he came back, he gave a royal dinner, and Benjamin was in the place of honor. But he still did not reveal to his brothers who he was.

He would try once more to discover whether the brothers who had once been willing to kill him and to plunge their father into grief, had learned since then to care for someone besides themselves.

Therefore he ordered his servants to fill all their sacks with grain, to put their money back in the mouth of their sacks, and in Benjamin's sack to put the silver cup that he himself liked most to drink from.

The next morning the sons of Jacob, including Simeon and Benjamin, started home. When they camped that night, they were overtaken by messengers from Egypt who accused them of having stolen Joseph's cup. They denied that they knew anything about it. Joseph's officers could open their sacks and see. So the sacks were opened one by one, and there was no sign that the owner of any of them was guilty. Then came the last sack, Benjamin's; and there concealed in Benjamin's sack was Joseph's cup.

The brothers rent their clothes, and in terror they went back to face the man in Egypt.

Joseph was still in his house when they got there. "What is this that you have done?" he demanded.

When they tried to answer, he told them what they could expect. Those who had not been shown to be guilty could go home. But the one in whose sack the cup had been found would stay there, a slave in Egypt. And that one was Benjamin, whom all the others, and particularly Judah, had pledged to bring home safe to their father.

Then Judah stood up and made his plea. "O my Lord," he said, "let not your anger burn against your servant. You asked us 'Have you a father or a brother?' And we said, 'We have a father, an old man, and a young brother, the child of his old age; and his brother is dead, and he alone is left of his mother's children, and his father loves him.' Then you said to your servants, 'Bring him down to me, that I may set my eyes upon him.' We said to my lord, 'The lad cannot leave his father, for if he should leave his father, his father would die.' "

Then Judah went on to tell of how they had gone back to Jacob, and persuaded him to let Benjamin come; and of how he, Judah, had promised his father to stand between Benjamin and any harm. "Now therefore," he said, "let your servant, I pray you, remain instead of the lad as a slave to my lord; and let the lad go back with his brothers."

Then Joseph's emotion welled up so within him that he could control himself no more. He sent all the Egyptian servants out of the room, lest he should weep before them. And he cried out to his brothers, "I am Joseph. Is my father still alive?"

They were too dismayed to answer him. And no wonder. For "the dreamer" whom they had derided was the man who now confronted them, in the place of power second only to Pharaoh's own.

But Joseph said, "Come near to me, I pray you"; and they came toward him. "I am your brother, Joseph, whom you sold into Egypt," he went on. "Now be not distressed, or angry with yourselves, because you sold me here. For God sent me before you to preserve life. So it was not you that sent me here but God."

He fell upon Benjamin's neck and kissed him; and he kissed all his brothers, and wept.

They should go back now, he said, and tell their father what had happened to his son, and they were to bring Jacob down to live in Egypt.

So the news was brought to Jacob, and his heart fainted because he could not believe what he was told. But when he knew that it was true, he said, "It is enough. Joseph, my son, is still alive; I will go and see him before I die."

Then Jacob and all his sons and their possessions came down into Egypt, and Pharaoh gave them land in the sheep country of Goshen.

Jacob lived to lay his hands in blessing on the heads of Joseph's sons, Ephraim and Manasseh; and when he died, Joseph carried his body and buried it in the cave of Machpelah, which Abraham had bought when he buried Sarah.

CHAPTER FOURTEEN

Trouble Falls Upon the Descendants of Jacob

<hr>

A s LONG as Joseph lived, all went well with the family of Jacob. But after Joseph had died, there came a new dynasty in Egypt. The Pharaohs who succeeded had no such interest in the descendants of Jacob as the Pharaoh of Joseph's time had had. Instead they grew suspicious of these Hebrew clans that now were settled within the Egyptian borders. Who knew whether in a period of war, or other danger, they might show themselves as aliens who could not be trusted, so the rulers of Egypt began to ask. And what they determined was to reduce these Hebrews, who called themselves the Children of Israel, to slave labor. Let them make the bricks from which the Pharaoh's store cities of Pithom and Rameses were being built, and let them do it under taskmasters who would not spare the lash.

It was in the 1200's b.c. (as closely as calculation can be made) that this was happening. Egypt then was one of the great empires of the world, with a rich civilization already long established. For more than fifteen hundred years the giant stone face of the Sphinx had looked out—as it still looks out—over the valley of the Nile; and centuries before the Sphinx the Pharaoh Khufu had devised for his tomb the vast pyramid at Gizeh, and had seen it lifted five hundred feet to its apex in stone blocks hewn to incredible precision in the quarries and dragged by ropes across the desert sands. The great cities of Thebes and Memphis had been built, and the colossal temples at Luxor and at Karnak. In the Valley of the Kings the bodies of successive Pharaohs had been laid in their

alabaster sarcophagi, surrounded by the treasures, the jewels and
the gold, such as met the astonished eyes of the excavators who in
1922 discovered and opened the tomb of Tut-ank-hamen. In the
fifteenth century B.C. the great Pharaoh Thothmes III had led
Egyptian armies north to the conquest of Syria, and beyond that
his invading chariots had rolled as far as the Euphrates River. In
the 1200's B.C. the Pharaoh was Rameses II who had fought successfully against the Hittite empire in Asia Minor and whose
colossal statues of himself, sixty-five feet high, stand by the portals
of the temple that he built at Abu Simbel.

Such was the Egypt in which the descendants of Jacob found
themselves at the period which was to be the beginning of the
supreme chapter in their history.

The Book of Genesis, which ends with the story of Joseph, reflects for the most part an age when the far-off facts were wrapped
in folklore, like a landscape seen only in glimpses through a morning mist. In the Book of Exodus, there are also elements of legend,
some of which were to become marvels in their subsequent
retelling. But in this Book of Exodus, the central narrative of
the Old Testament moves into the period of clearer history, and in
that history one great and decisive figure emerges. His name was
Moses.

When he was born, the people of Israel were in the depths of
their distress. All through the centuries the Egyptian Pharaohs
had had a cruel contempt for human life, when human lives had
to be the cost for what they wanted to accomplish. The pyramids
could never have been built except by the killing labor of conscripted tens-of-thousands who were driven until they dropped.
And now when the new Pharaoh, who may have been Rameses,
chose to build his treasure cities, it made no difference to him
what happened to Israelites who were forced to build them. If
they could not be made into convenient labor, they had as well be
dead. In fact in some of his moods it seemed to the Pharaoh that
if most of these Israelites should die, that would be all the better,
for then they would no longer be a possible menace in the land of

Jacob's vision at Bethel of a ladder between heaven and earth.

Joseph's envious brothers sell him as a slave.

Egypt. So the first chapter of the Book of Exodus tells that at one time the Pharaoh ordered that all male babies of the Israelites should be killed.

Against that background the story of Moses begins.

He was born to the wife of a man of the tribe of Levi, who hid him for three months from any officer of Pharaoh who might have found him. But the time came when she could not hide him in her house any longer. She made a little basket out of bulrushes, made it water-tight with pitch, and put it among the tall reeds by the bank of the Nile. And she told her little daughter, the baby's sister, to stay near and watch.

Down to the river, who should come to bathe, but the daughter of Pharaoh. As she walked by the water's edge, she saw the tiny basket. She sent one of her maids to take it up and to bring it to her. And when she opened it, there was the baby. When the baby cried, the heart of the princess melted. "This is one of the Hebrew children," she said. But whoever this baby was, she was going to keep him.

Just then the little girl standing near, who was the baby's sister, spoke to the princess. Would she like her to go and find one of the women of the Hebrews to be the baby's nurse? Yes, she would. So the child went off and brought her own mother, and the daughter of Pharaoh told the mother to take care of him until she was ready to have him herself. Presently she was ready, and she took him to grow up as her own son. And it was she who called him Moses, "Because," she said, "I drew him out of the water."

So the boy who was born of the Hebrews was growing up in all the rich privilege of Pharaoh's court. But meanwhile, the lot of his people was growing worse and worse, until their lives were bitter with hard service.

The years went by and Moses was grown. One day he went out where the men of Israel were being driven to work. He saw an Egyptian overseer lash one of them with his whip. Adopted son of Pharaoh's daughter or not, he was of the same blood as that beaten man. He sprang upon the Egyptian overseer, struck him down, and killed him.

CHAPTER FIFTEEN

Moses Is Called
as the Deliverer

THE REPORT of what Moses had done began to spread. When
the word was brought to Pharaoh that someone had killed
one of the taskmasters he had set over the Hebrews, he was furious.
Moses did not dare to stay in Egypt.

He fled into the rough country of Midian where a fugitive could
not easily be traced. Coming one day to a well, he found some
girls there trying to draw water for their sheep; but shepherds
of another flock pushed in ahead of them. The same quick anger
against what was mean and brutal that had swept over Moses
when he saw the overseer in Egypt, flared within him now. He
drove the shepherds off and drew water for the other flock.

The girls went back and told their father, Jethro, who was head
of one of the desert tribes. "Why did you leave the man?" he said.
"Where is he? Go and call him."

So Moses was brought to Jethro's tents, and stayed there. After
a while he married one of Jethro's daughters; and it might have
seemed that the rest of his life would drift along without notice
there in Midian, out of all connection with the passions that were
boiling up in Egypt. In the land of Pharaoh the oppression of the
Hebrews was continually more heavy. They were ordered to make
bricks; and when, in their exhaustion, they failed to make the
number that had been required, the overseers had no mercy. Not
only should these Hebrews meet the first demands. They should
have new demands laid on them. Before this, they had been given
the straw to mix in with the clay. Now they were to be responsible

for getting their own straw, and yet make no fewer bricks. "And their cry came up to God by reason of their bondage."

The rumor of all this may have been carried as far as Midian. What, if anything, should Moses do?

One day as he led the flock of Jethro in the country near Mount Horeh, while the sun blazed down he saw a bush that was shimmering with fire. Yet the bush was not consumed. And as Moses stopped and gazed in wonder, the burning bush turned into the vision of an angel, and Moses heard the voice of God. "Put off your shoes from your feet, for the place on which you are standing is holy ground. I am the God of your father, the God of Abraham, the God of Isaac, and the God of Jacob." And Moses hid his face, for he was afraid of the presence of God.

Then the voice went on, "I have seen the affliction of my people who are in Egypt, and have heard their cry because of their taskmasters. I know their sufferings, and I have come down to deliver them out of the hand of the Egyptians. I will send you to Pharaoh that you may bring forth my people, the sons of Israel, out of Egypt."

"I will send you!"—that was the awful commission that Moses heard. *He* must go and confront Pharaoh. *He* must be the leader of an enslaved people and lead them from the power of Egypt; this unarmed and helpless people from the Egypt whose magnificence and might had builded the temples and the pyramids and clothed its Pharaohs in awful majesty! "Who am I," he cried to God, "that I should go to Pharaoh, and bring the sons of Israel out of Egypt?"

Then came the long struggle between Moses' human shrinking and the divine compulsion that had laid hold of him and from which there was no escape.

"They will not believe me or listen to my voice," said Moses.

"I am not eloquent, either heretofore or since thou hast spoken to thy servant," he pleaded again; "but I am slow of speech and of tongue."

Each time the voice of God answered him. God would be with him, and would show the signs of his sufficient power. And as to Moses' eloquence or lack of it, the answer came again. "Who has made man's mouth? Who makes him dumb, or deaf, or seeing, or blind? Is it not I, the Lord? Now therefore go, and I will be with your mouth and teach you what you shall speak."

Stripped now of all his reasons, Moses could only cry abjectly, "Oh, my Lord, send, I pray you, some other person!" And for that moment of weakness, he should pay a weary price. For the voice of God replied that if Moses had to be so hesitant, Aaron, his brother, should go with him to be the spokesman. And Aaron did afterwards go, to help Moses in some ways, and to be a trial and vexation in other and more ways.

When the vision of the burning bush was finished, Moses knew what he had to do. No matter what he feared, he must go back to Egypt. Thinking of all the gods worshipped in the temples there, he had begged God in his vision to tell him the special name of God whose awful demand he should present to Pharaoh. But the answer had come, *"I am who I am."* The greatness of God should be shown not in words, but in what he was about to do.

Down to Egypt then Moses went, and Aaron with him. They gathered together all the elders of the people of Israel, and told

them that they had come at the divine command. Then they went
to the court of Pharaoh. And what must have been the amazement
and the indignation of Pharaoh as he listened to the words they
dared to speak, "Thus says the Lord, the God of Israel, 'Let my
people go!' "

"Who is this Lord that I should heed his voice and let Israel
go?" Pharaoh demanded; and there they stood face to face, Moses
perilously back from exile, and the king of Egypt.

Now began the events that in the memory of Israel were to be
lifted up like a mighty mountain range above the level of common life, and from which immemorial influences would flow to
change all the face of history. A captive people was asserting its
will to live, against the tyranny of one of the world's great empires. Its spokesman, unarmed and unprotected, confronted the
ruler who had servants and armed guards and prisons ready at his
word. Yet, in spite of everything, the enslaved people were to win
their freedom. They should inherit a country of their own, and
in that country create the Holy City of a new spiritual witness on
the earth. So it is no wonder that in the chronicles of Israel, and
in the faith of the Jewish people to the end of time, what happened in Egypt was seen as no less than supernatural. It was not a
matter only of a collision of will between two human beings,
Moses and the king of Egypt; for in that collision Moses by himself was helpless. Above that apparent duel a mightier force was
working. The will of an Eternal Righteousness, the purpose of
God himself, for history was opening a new era of revelation of
the power of the Unseen.

The great marvel was the fact in actual history that Israel did
go free. It was no wonder then that the setting of it, and all its
crucial scenes, were dramatized in the tradition. The result was
like a miracle. How could it be described then except in terms of
miracles? So the narrative in the Book of Exodus tells of magicians
at Pharaoh's court who tried to show their magic and of Moses
confounding them with greater signs. And it tells of disasters
which fell upon the land, and ultimately made Pharaoh weaken,

as having come through the direct instrumentality of Moses as the spokesman for God. In the seventh chapter of the Book of Exodus, therefore, begins the story of the plagues of Egypt.

The Lord said to Moses, "Pharaoh's heart is hardened, he refuses to let the people go. Go to Pharaoh in the morning, as he is going out to the water; wait for him by the river's brink, and take in your hand your rod which was turned into a serpent. And you shall say to him, 'The Lord, the God of the Hebrews, sent me to you, saying, "Let my people go, that they may serve me in the wilderness, and behold, you have not obeyed." Thus says the Lord, "By this you shall know that I am the Lord: behold, I will strike the water that is in the Nile with the rod that is in my hand, and it shall be turned to blood, and the fish in the Nile shall die, and the Nile shall become foul, and the Egyptians will loathe to drink water from the Nile.' "

Then it happened as Moses had declared. The water of the river grew thick and stagnant with the red mud that filled it, so that the fish died in it, and it was no longer fit for men to drink. But Pharaoh turned his back, went into his house and would not listen.

In relentless succession came the other plagues.

Frogs swarmed up out of the river and the canals, frogs that hopped and slithered everywhere, over the fields, in the courtyards, and in the houses. When the frogs died, the land was filled with the stench of them, so that even Pharaoh could not stand it, and he said to Moses and Aaron that if they could prevail upon the Lord to take away the plague of frogs he would let the people of Israel go.

But when the plague did abate, Pharaoh changed his mind. Moses may not have had anything to do with the frogs' coming in the first place, or with their going either. So why should he pay attention to this man's insolent demands? The people of Israel could keep on at their work.

Consequently, other plagues had to follow. First, there was a cloud of gnats that tormented men and beasts. Then there were

flies, swarming over people's faces and crawling on their food; and
after the flies a disease that began to kill the camels, and the cattle,
and the flocks of sheep.

Still Pharaoh held out. Even worse would have to happen before his resistance could be broken.

Moses took handfuls of ashes from a kiln and threw the ashes
into the air in front of Pharaoh. What new punishment did that
foretoken? Pharaoh was soon to find out. On all the people of
Egypt boils began to break out. Pharaoh sent for his magicians to
work some spell that would end the boils, but the magicians themselves had to send word to Pharaoh that their own boils were so
bad that they could not stand up.

Once more the word of warning must be conveyed to Pharaoh.
Moses stood before him. "Thus says the Lord, the God of the
Hebrews," he repeated; " 'Let my people go!' "

Over all the land hail began to fall, with thunder, and lightning
flashing in the midst of the hail—heavy hail, such as had never
been seen in Egypt since it became a nation. And the hail struck
down everything that was in the fields, both man and beast, and
shattered even trees. And after the hail came swarms of locusts, so
thick that the sky was darkened. They ate the few late crops that
the hail had not destroyed, so that not a green thing was left in all
the land.

Now panic began to spread among the common people. How
long must these deadly plagues go on? Couldn't Pharaoh understand that Egypt was being ruined?

At last Pharaoh himself was forced to see that something must
be done. He would grant a little of what Moses had demanded but
not much. "Your people want to go out of Egypt to worship your
God," he said to Moses. But who did Moses mean by "the people"?
Who did he think would be allowed to go?

Everybody, Moses said. "Our young and our old; our sons and
daughters, our flocks and herds."

No! "Drive him out!" said Pharaoh to his servants. What this
Moses was demanding was too much to be listened to. Some of
the men of the Israelites might go out for the worship in the

desert they were bent upon. But the women and children should stay in Egypt—which was Pharaoh's assurance that the men would come back.

That was not enough for Moses. All the people of Israel must go free.

Over the land of Egypt there fell a thick darkness, so that men groped their way about. Pharaoh, instead of surrendering, grew the more defiant. "Get away from me!" he said to Moses. "Take heed to yourself. Never see my face again; for if you do, you shall die."

And Moses answered, "As you say! I will not see your face again."

CHAPTER SIXTEEN

The Exodus from Egypt

THEN CAME the last and most dreadful of the visitations upon Pharaoh and his kingdom. Terrible as it was, it seemed to the chroniclers of Israel to be no more than the cruelty of Egypt had deserved. And so it was told from generation to generation, and written in the Book of Exodus, as the coming of an avenging angel of the Lord.

Moses went out for the last time from the presence of Pharaoh. He gathered the elders of Israel and he told them that in that month of Nisan every household should take an unblemished lamb; and on the fourteenth day of the month the lambs should be sacrificed, and some of the blood from each household's lamb be sprinkled on the door posts of the house. That night destruction should pass through the land, and in every Egyptian family the first-born would die; but every house that was marked with the blood of the lambs should be safe.

Moreover, Moses told the people that on that evening they should be ready for the great deliverance which God would work. They were to make their supper of the roasted lambs and of unleavened bread; and they were to eat it hastily, with their sandals on their feet, their loins girded, and all things set for immediate departure. This should be the hour for their escape from Egypt.

Then the night came and with it the stroke that was to break the will of Pharaoh. "At midnight," says the twelfth chapter of the Book of Exodus, "the Lord smote the first-born in the land of Egypt, from the first-born of Pharaoh who sat on his throne to the first-born of the captive who was in the dungeon, and all the first-born of the cattle. And Pharaoh rose up in the night, he, and all his servants, and all the Egyptians; and there was a great cry in Egypt, for there was not a house where there was not one dead. And he summoned Moses and Aaron by night, and said, 'Rise up, go forth from among my people, both you and the people of Israel' . . . And the Egyptians were urgent with the people, to send them out of the land in haste; for they said 'We are all dead men.' "

And what had happened on that last night, according to the immemorial tradition, was the origin and the meaning of the Feast of the Passover, which would be celebrated century after century by all faithful Jews in the spring month of Nisan, the first month of the Jewish year. It is the Passover because it was written in the Book of Exodus that on the night of deliverance from Egypt, when the blood of the lambs had been sprinkled on the doors, this had been the promise of the Lord, "The blood shall be a sign for you, upon the houses where you are; and when I see the blood I will pass over you, and no plague shall fall upon you to destroy you, when I smite the land of Egypt." And the sacredness of the Passover was expressed also in the words ascribed to Moses, "Remember this day, in which you came out from Egypt, out of the house of bondage, for by strength of hand the Lord brought you out from this place. And when your children say to you, 'What do you mean by this service?' you shall say, 'It is the sacrifice of the Lord's Passover, for he passed over the houses of the people of Israel in Egypt, when he slew the Egyptians and spared our houses.' "

After they had eaten the Passover supper, the people rallied to the leadership of Moses around the city of Rameses, and began to move toward the Egyptian borders. The long years of ignominy seemed to be over. They were moving out to find their destiny as a free people in the Promised Land.

The succession of disasters that had fallen upon Egypt had been too much even for Pharaoh. He had let the people of Israel go. But his anger and his outraged pride flamed up again. These slaves of his had thought they could escape. But they were not yet beyond his reach. He ordered the horses harnessed to his chariots, and he set out in pursuit.

The throng of Israelites, with women and children and their flocks and herds, could move only at the pace of the weakest and the slowest. Feet dragged as the night went on. The people looked back anxiously at the road behind them, in fear that Pharaoh's chariots would be coming. And the fear turned into fact. From a camp where the tired multitude had had to stop, a fateful cloud of dust grew visible. It was the dust from the hoofs of Pharaoh's on-coming horses.

Now it would be apparent how nearly the spirit of the people had been broken in their years of bondage, and how great would be the task for Moses' leadership. The people cried to Moses, "Is it because there are no graves in Egypt that you have taken us away to die in the wilderness? It would have been better for us to serve the Egyptians than to die."

But Moses said, "Fear not, stand firm, and see the salvation of the Lord"; and Moses heard the voice of God, "Tell the people of Israel to go forward."

Then came the incredible deliverance that was to be put into unending song and story. Faced with a shallow arm of the sea, the Israelites at Moses' command went into it as a strong east wind blew aside the water and made a line of passage. The pursuing chariots of Pharaoh drove in after them. But the wind changed and the waters flooded back, and chariots and horsemen were caught and overwhelmed.

No wonder then that in the fifteenth chapter of Exodus there is the triumphant chant which begins, "The Lord is my strength and song, and he is become my salvation," and goes on to its climactic cry of faith, "The Lord will reign for ever and ever."

CHAPTER SEVENTEEN

Moses at Mount Sinai

T HE REGION into which the Israelites had to go in their escape
was harsh and inhospitable country. They could not go north
along the seaboard of the Mediterranean, because there were
Egyptian forts that would have barred their way. Consequently,
if they were to reach the land of Canaan they had to go a round-
about way; eastward and then far south through the barren penin-
sula of Sinai, before they could turn northward at length toward
entrance into Canaan, as it were by the back door. On their route
they would find little food and sometimes less water. Around them
towered bleak granite mountains, desolate and menacing and
empty of sustenance for man or beast.

The faint-hearted among the people began to break into bitter
lamentation. Life in Egypt had been bad, but now the hardships
in the desert seemed worse. In the valley of the Nile, with the
great river flowing and wells of water even in the desert sands, they
would at least never die of thirst. And in the fields of Egypt there

was grain. But where were they now? Stumbling on across the endless stretches of sand and gravel, where the relentless sun beat down by day, and where at night a sudden chill fell as the sun went down behind gigantic mountains and their long shadows fell across the desert plain.

At first the route that Moses chose led southward along the Suez shore. Then it turned inland, and in all the tawny and naked desert the only water they came upon was a pool so foul that the complaining people called it Marah, which meant the place of bitter waters. But Moses had been in this wilderness before. He knew that there were leaves of a particular plant which would help clear the pool; he found some of these and made the water fit to drink.

Along with thirst went hunger. What little food the people had been able to bring from Egypt was soon gone. Then they began to think that, in comparison with this, Egypt was like a lost paradise. They told one another that in Egypt "we sat by the fleshpots and ate bread to the full." Now they faced starvation.

But even when things seemed at their worst, there came deliverance, as though it had dropped down from the sky. One day a great covey of quails, exhausted from their flight over the Gulf of Suez, alighted on the desert so spent that the Israelites could

catch them in their hands. And in the mornings they discovered on the sands a sweet white gum that fell with the dew from the leaves of tamarisk bushes. When the sun was up, it melted; but if it was gathered early, it was good food. The people called it manna; but Moses said, "It is the bread which the Lord has given you to eat."

Scarcity of food and water was not the only danger that the Israelites encountered in the desert. The new danger burst upon them just when they had come to what men in the arid wilderness crave for most—an oasis. Here and there, even in the worst deserts, subterranean waters bubble to the surface and make a green garden spot of springs and grass and palm trees. But because an oasis is so precious, it may be fought for fiercely by the desert tribes. Scarcely had the fugitives from Egypt arrived at this oasis when they were attacked by the Amalakites. All day the battle raged, while Moses—with Aaron and Hur helping to hold up his hands—invoked the help of God. By sundown the attacking tribesmen were beaten off; but even so the oasis was not a place where the Israelites could stay. Moses led them further, up toward the awesome heights of Mount Sinai.

Now come the chapters in the Book of Exodus which give the story of the flight from Egypt its immortal meaning. The escape of a band of Hebrew fugitives from their obscure bondage might have seemed in itself of trivial consequence for the world at large. But among this people was the towering figure who brought to them a consciousness of something mightier than the things of earth. Moses had not lost his vision of the burning bush. He believed that his own life, and the life of Israel, were part of an almighty purpose. This fugitive people should be bound into a community, the strength of which should come not through mortal facts but through faith in the living God. And the God whose voice had first come to him in his vision, and in whose name he had dared to confront Pharaoh, was not like the gods of Egypt nor like any of the other tribal gods who were supposed to want a kind of worship directed to impulses and appetites like those of men. What God desired most was not a sacrificial code but upright conduct, not quantity of offerings but a new quality of life.

Moses left the people camped at the foot of Sinai and he climbed up alone into the mountain's awful solitude. He had led the people this far on the road of hoped-for freedom. What should he try to make them understand as to the purpose they must follow and the faith that they must keep?

Then to his mind and soul there came the word of God, "You have seen what I did to the Egyptians, and how I bore you on eagles' wings and brought you to myself. Now, therefore, if you will obey my voice and keep my covenant, you shall be my own possession among all peoples; for all the earth is mine, and you shall be to me a kingdom of priests and a holy nation."

"A kingdom of priests and a holy nation." So this people could have greatness not in possessions, but in being a witness among the nations to the will of the living God.

And what was his will? Down from the mountain, at the end of his lonely vigil, Moses came—bringing the answer—inscribed on two tablets of stone. And the answer was the Ten Commandments:

I am the Lord thy God; Thou shalt have none other gods but me.

Thou shalt not make to thyself any graven image, nor the likeness of anything that is in heaven above, or in the earth beneath, or in the water under the earth; thou shalt not bow down to them, nor worship them.

Thou shalt not take the Name of the Lord thy God in vain.

Remember that thou keep holy the Sabbath day.

Honor thy father and thy mother.

Thou shalt do no murder.

Thou shalt not commit adultery.

Thou shalt not steal.

Thou shalt not bear false witness against thy neighbor.

Thou shalt not covet.

In those Ten Commandments was the standard which should not only judge the life of Israel, but should become inescapable for the general conscience of mankind. In the first four Commandments is the call to human souls to give their devotion to the Eternal Righteousness; in the last six, the truth that real worship must regulate and purify men's behavior toward one another. Here in "The Two Tables of the Law," religion and morality have been forever linked.

But while Moses was on the mountain something different was happening in the valley. The hours had gone by, and Moses had not re-appeared. In the meantime, a terrifying storm had broken with lightning flashing and the thunder crashing on the heights of Sinai and re-echoing in its dark ravines. What had become of Moses? No one knew. Uneasiness and fear began to spread, and in that mood whatever faith the people might have had was disappearing. A crowd of them went to Aaron. "Get up," they said, "and make us gods. As for this Moses, the man who brought us out of the land of Egypt, we do not know what has become of him."

Now Moses was coming down. Some time before, Joshua had left the camp and had gone up into the mountain to look for Moses, and had found him. To the ears of them both a noise came up from below—the noise of shouting and singing arose from the crowd. Fighting must have broken out, said Joshua. But Moses said it did not sound like fighting, not like shouts of victory or cries of defeat. It was some kind of singing.

And so it was. When Moses and Joshua came where they could see, there below them the people were dancing around something set up in their midst. And when they came nearer still, they saw that the something was an idol. The people had demanded of Aaron that he make them an image like one of the bull-gods of Egypt. He had made one, and in wild relapse to any superstition that they thought might save them, the people were bringing their offerings to "the molten calf."

Now the anger of Moses blazed until it seemed as terrible as the thunder-storm on Sinai. He flung down the tablets of stone on which the Commandments had been written. He took the image of the calf, threw it into the fire, ground it to pieces in the ashes, and then poured the dust of it into water and made the people drink. Then he confronted Aaron like the avenging wrath of God. "What did this people do to you that you have brought this great sin upon them?" he demanded.

Like many another man caught in the consequence of moral weakness, Aaron tried to crawl out under the cover of excuses. He did not start the trouble; somebody else did. "You know the people," he said, "that they are set on evil." *They* had insisted "Make us gods, who shall go before us," and they had said that they did not know what had become of Moses. So all that he did, Aaron tried to say, was that he had replied to the people that if they had any gold they should bring it to him. "So they gave it to me, and I threw it into the fire, and there came out this calf."

What would happen now? The tablets of stone on which the Commandments were inscribed had been broken when Moses in his indignation flung them down. They could be inscribed again; but how and when could they be written in the heart of this people who were so slow to learn?

The Book of Exodus, like the other Books that deal with the beginnings of Old Testament history, gathered together the many traditions that had come down. Some of these may reflect not so much the exact occurrences as what men of very human impulses supposed must rightly have occurred. So in one passage it is related that as punishment for what the people had done Moses stood at the entrance of the camp and called "Who is on the Lord's side? Come to me." And when the men of his own tribe of Levi gathered about him, he made them take their swords and go through the camp and kill some of the guilty ones, until three thousand men were slain.

But directly after that account there comes another passage which is much more revealing of the reality that made Moses great; for his greatness was not in reflecting human passions but in trying to understand the redemptiveness of God. So he said to the people, "You have sinned a great sin. And now I will go up to the Lord; perhaps I can make atonement for your sin."

He went away therefore and prayed. He confessed the people's guilt. He begged that they might be forgiven. If not, then he was ready to be linked with their condemnation. "If not, blot me," he said, "out of thy book." And after that comes a description of how Moses went again up on Mount Sinai in order that he might bring back new tables of the Law; and on the mountain "the Lord descended in the cloud," and made known to Moses that, not withstanding the guilt of men, God is at last "merciful and gracious, slow to anger, and abounding in steadfast love and faithfulness, forgiving iniquity and transgression and sin."

CHAPTER EIGHTEEN

The Brave,
and the Fainthearted

I N THE Book of Exodus, and particularly in the Books of Leviticus and Numbers which follow, there are long chapters in
which the Old Testament may seem very far from a "living story."
They have to do with laws and regulations which are not the timeless principles of religion and life such as the Ten Commandments, but instead are the minute prescriptions laid down for a
people in the primitive conditions of a desert journey centuries
ago. Some of the regulations had to do with the raw facts of everyday existence—with how to keep the camp clean, how to prevent
disease, what to do with dead bodies. Many of them had to do with
the innumerable causes for disagreement and controversy, with
damage done to somebody's possessions and with what had to be
paid, with quarrels and violence and a summary justice which
sometimes meant "an eye for an eye and a tooth for a tooth." And
there are long and elaborate descriptions of how the Israelites were
supposed to have worshipped in the wilderness—of a tabernacle,
richly adorned, set up as the central tent in every encampment,
and of the sacred ark that belonged within it.

All these laws and prescriptions were ascribed to Moses, and the
impression of his great personality may indeed be upon those central laws which were laid down for the people's daily life and conduct. On the other hand, much of what the ancient compilers set
forth as the Mosaic Code was the gradual reflection of community
experience for a world long gone, and for conditions of a vanished
time. One does not have to linger, therefore, over the minutiae

74

in Exodus and Leviticus. The express words, even of the Ten Commandments, may or may not have come through Moses. But what emerges from the narrative is the man himself, who in his unconquerable spirit brought to a whole people a consciousness of the living God.

It was a long way yet from Sinai to the Promised Land, and the strength of will that would be needed for advance must come continually from Moses. As the story of the march through the wilderness was told and re-told through many generations, it began to be seen through the perspective of glamorous tradition. So it was written afterward in the Book of Numbers that there was a cloud over the tabernacle by day and "at even the appearance of fire"—as also in the Book of Exodus it was written that the people had been guided by cloud and fire when they came first to the crossing of the Red Sea. So the chroniclers symbolized the truth that in the deliverance of Israel a guidance greater than the accidents of earth was working. And the instrument through which that guidance came was the man to whom the voice of God had said in the beginning, "Certainly, I will be with you, and will teach you what you shall do."

At one of the encampments, the old complaints about the hardships in the desert country broke out again. Not all the people were trouble-makers, but there was a rabble who always were. Instead of looking ahead, they looked back; loud with whining lamentation. It was not this way in Egypt, they said, and it would be better to be back in Egypt than out in this country where even a camel could hardly find enough to live on. "We remember the fish we ate in Egypt," they said, "and the cucumbers, the leeks, the onions, and the melons. Now our strength is dried up."

These mutterings among the crowd were bad enough to have to deal with, but a harder trial also came to Moses. Aaron, his brother, and Miriam, his sister, began to talk against him. Why should Moses think he was the only one who knew the mind of the Lord? Couldn't the Lord speak to *them* as well as he could to Moses? So they were starting whispers that might undermine his leadership.

Shortly after this there appeared on Miriam the white spots that could be the awful sign of leprosy; and those who saw it said that it must be a punishment from God. But Moses' only impulse was to plead with God for Miriam's healing; and in the Book of Numbers is the revealing comment, "Now the man Moses was very meek, more than all men that were on the face of the earth."

Moses meek? Pharaoh certainly did not think so. Aaron certainly had not thought so, that day when Moses came down from the mountain and in blazing indignation destroyed the golden calf. Moses had seemed as terrible as the lightning bolts on Sinai. How could he who had been so formidable and so dominant be also meek?

Yet the fact was that he could be both. It depended upon what he was confronted with. When God's purpose was at stake, then the man's whole spirit could be the channel for a divine and holy wrath. He could confront evil with the awful power of a heavenly righteousness, because he was lifted above all self-interest and self-regard. But this same man who could make God's judgments so irresistible, could be humble and patient when it was not God's cause but only his own prestige that was concerned. He was great enough to distinguish the great things from the small. So when men resisted God, he could be terrible; but when they only slighted him, he could treat that as a trivial thing. Long afterwards it would be said by one greater than Moses, "Blessed are the meek, for they shall inherit the earth." And it was because of Moses' kind of meekness, self-controlled, long-suffering, resolute, that the people of Israel could be led at last to the Promised Land.

Notwithstanding the difficulties that had to be dealt with, the slow advance continued, and the time came when the Israelites had reached the borders of Canaan. Now the question was whether they could go in and occupy the land.

Moses sent scouts ahead. "See what the land is," he told them, "and whether the people who dwell in it are strong or weak, whether they are few or many, and whether the land that they dwell in is good or bad and whether they live in encampments or in fortified towns. Be of good courage, and bring some of the fruit of the land."

So the scouts went out, twelve of them. Then they came back and made their reports.

The reports were as opposite as day and night. All the scouts had seen the same things, but they had looked at them with different eyes, because they were two different kinds of men.

All twelve agreed that it was a good land, fertile and inviting. But ten men said that the Israelites could not hope to win it because the people who held it were too strong. The more they told about them, the more they expanded their story of how fearsome those people were. Before they finished, they had made them out as giants. Measured against them, they said, "We seemed to ourselves like grasshoppers."

Two of the scouts, Caleb and Joshua, protested hotly against what the ten had said. To say that the people in Canaan were like giants meant nothing except to show what they had seemed to the eyes of cowards. They were no more than ordinary people. "Stop being afraid of them," they said. "The Lord is with us. Do not fear."

But part of the crowd in the camp that heard the report of the scouts turned into a frightened mob. "We wish we had died in the land of Egypt," they exclaimed; "or died in the wilderness. Why does the Lord bring us into this land to fall by the sword? Our wives and our little ones will become prey. It would be better for us to go back to Egypt."

Out of the crowd then came even the cry of mutiny—"Let us choose a captain, and go back to Egypt!"

But there was no captain to lead them. The ugly commotion died down in the face of the courage of Caleb and Joshua and the resolution of Moses. But the immediate chance to enter Canaan had been thrown away. Long years must go by, until the generation which had been slaves in Egypt had died off, and a new and hardier lot grown up to take their place.

CHAPTER NINETEEN

Moses Leads
the People Through

THE EXODUS out of Egypt was not the march of a trained army. It was the migration of mixed people, women and children as well as men. So, at the best, it could make its way ahead only with painful slowness. In addition to that, there was the faint-heartedness and the near-rebellion by which Moses was confronted from among the weaker sort. The Old Testament record speaks repeatedly of "forty years" in the wilderness. In the language of Israel, forty was a round number that could be used for a time indefinitely long, which yet had been long enough to seem unending. It is not likely that forty calendar years went by in the people's journeying; but whatever the period of years, at the end of it there had developed men who could respond to courageous leadership.

On the way toward Canaan the Israelites by-passed the hostile tribes of Edom as they made their way north toward the mountains of Moab that look down from the east upon the grim chasm of the Dead Sea. But beyond the river Arnon lay the country of the Amorites whose "king," or tribal chief, was Sihon. Messengers were sent out to Sihon, asking that Israel might pass through his land peaceably. They would go, they promised, only by the beaten paths; they would not set foot on any of the Amorites' fields or vineyards, or even drink water from their wells. Sihon sent back a blunt refusal. Not only that; he armed his tribesmen and they rode out to the attack.

But the men whom Sihon encountered were better fighters than he had imagined. His Amorites were beaten; and the Israelites took possession not only of the road they had wanted in the first place, but of the Amorite country around it. Nor did they stop there. They crossed the river Jabbok and routed the tribesmen of Og, who was called "the king of Bashan."

The fighting men of Israel now had a new confidence in themselves, and fear of them began to spread among all the peoples in the border country to the east of the Dead Sea and the Jordan River. Around the campfires of Israel the exultant spirit broke into spontaneous singing that grew into rhythmic chants, fragments of which have come down from what is otherwise a lost and forgotten "Book of the Wars of the Lord." And incidents were happening round about that grew in the retelling as dramatic imagination looked back upon the original fact as upon a mountain wrapped in a magnifying mist. So in the Book of Numbers one comes upon the wonder-tale of Balak and of Balaam, in which is expressed the conviction of Israel that the deliverance from Egypt was so divinely destined that no power could resist it, and that if anybody did, even a beast could tell him better.

Balak, king of Moab, was one of those who heard the ominous news of what had happened to Sihon and the Amorites, and to Og of Bashan. He wanted to get hold of somebody who could work enchantment, and he was told of a seer named Balaam, who was reputed to have some kind of magic power. He sent a message to him that there had come up out of Egypt a people that "cover the face of the earth," and they were at the borders of Balak's country. He wanted Balaam to come and put a curse upon them. And he sent enough money as a persuasive fee.

Balaam said he would think about it. But after he had said his prayers, he announced that he would not go.

The messengers of Balak returned to him; and Balak sent back some new representatives of higher rank than the first ones. They were to say to Balaam, "Let nothing hinder you from coming." Balak would treat him with great honor, and do whatever Balaam said; only come and curse these Israelites.

Balaam started to refuse again, and then he managed to conclude from his divinations that perhaps the signs were right, after all, for him to go. "So Balaam rose early in the morning, and saddled his ass, and went with the princes of Moab."

Then—as the tellers of the story interpreted it in Israel—"God's anger was kindled because he went; and the angel of the Lord took his stand in the way."

Balaam was riding on his ass, and his two servants were with him. If Balaam did not see the angel—or did not want to—the ass did see him, and turned off into the field. Angrily Balaam beat the ass and at length the ass went on to where the road narrowed to a path between vineyards, with a wall on either side. There again was the angel, and the ass swerved aside and mashed Balaam's foot against the wall, which made him beat the ass again.

And now the ass began to speak. Why was Balaam beating her?

Yes, he was beating her, Balaam answered; he only wished he had a sword in his hand so that he could strike her dead for being so stubborn.

But now even Balaam's eyes were opened. He saw the angel and he bowed his head, and fell on his face. Then what he heard from the angel was that he should go on with the men who had been sent to bring him; but that when he came to Balak he was to say only what God would tell him to say.

When Balak heard that Balaam was coming, he went out to meet him, and he offered a sacrifice of oxen and sheep. The next morning he took Balaam up on a bare hilltop, from which the camp of Israel could be seen. Now Balaam could curse these enemies of Balak. But to Balak's astonishment and outrage, what he heard Balaam say was this:

> How can I curse whom God has not cursed?
> How can I denounce whom the Lord has not denounced?
> Who can count the dust of Jacob,
>   or number the fourth part of Israel?
> Let me die the death of the righteous,
>   and let my end be like his.

"What have you done to me?" Balak demanded. "I took you to curse my enemies, and you have done nothing but bless them!"

Balaam said he had to speak what the Lord put in his mouth.

Balak took Balaam to two more places overlooking the tents of Israel, to try to get him to launch his curse. But it was no use. And at last when Balaam started back to his own country, to Balak's fierce anger and disgust, Balaam uttered a blessing upon Israel beyond any that he had spoken before.

> The oracle of Balaam the son of Beor,
>   the oracle of the man whose eye is opened,
>   who sees the vision of the Almighty
>   falling down, but having his eyes uncovered:
> A star shall come forth out of Jacob,
>   and a sceptre shall rise out of Israel.

That was the end of Balak's effort to get Balaam to work some sort of evil spell; and for the people of Israel the moral of the story was what they were coming boldly to believe—that nothing could finally stand in their way to keep them out of Canaan.

Not long afterwards Moses took a census of the people. Caleb and Joshua, the two scouts who had urged an assault on Canaan long before, were still living. The ten other scouts, the faint-hearted ones, were dead; and dead also were many of those who had been continually complaining in the wilderness. Perhaps the time had come for the decisive stroke.

But Moses was not to direct it. A younger man must take his place. Moses turned to Joshua, the son of Nun—the same Joshua who had been with him that day when he came down from Mount Sinai, and the same Joshua who had gone out with Caleb to scout the land of Canaan. He brought Joshua out before all the people, and he had the priest Eliezer lay his hands on Joshua as a sign of commission from the Lord.

At the end of the narrative of the Book of Numbers Moses was still alive, and still the leader and law-giver. But at the end of the Book of Deuteronomy, which belongs to a later date, there is the account of Moses' death, which lifts him up like an immortal figure belonging less to the earth than to the sky. When death came, it was to find him not upon the plains but upon a mountain. Up to the rocky height of Pisgah Moses went, on the great escarpment of the mountains of Moab that look down three thousand feet to the Dead Sea and the long trough of the Jordan River. There on the other side of the Jordan were the walls of Jericho, with palm trees and gardens around it; and beyond Jordan the hills and valleys of the land which had been the goal of his desire ever since he had stood before Pharaoh and demanded in the name of God, "Let my people go!" Now the people should enter upon their inheritance; and though he was not to enter with them, he had looked upon the Promised Land "while his eye was not dim, nor his natural force abated." And when he died, he was buried, as was fitting, there on the lonely grandeur of the mountain, and "no man knows the place of his burial to this day."

CHAPTER TWENTY

Jericho Captured, and Sisera Slain

T HE FIRST five Books of the Old Testament, together called the Pentateuch, were lifted in the thought of Israel to supreme authority as the *Torah,* or the Law. Here were the traditions as to the beginnings of life and of families and nations; and of the covenant established by God which had made Israel his chosen instrument. Here were not only the Ten Commandments but all the intricate regulations for daily life and conduct—as to what to eat or not to eat, as to how the hands should ritually be washed, as to what could or could not be done on weekdays and on the sabbath—which were attributed to Moses and believed to have come as the word of God through him. To this "Mosaic code" and to its observance the Jewish people would ultimately give unparalleled devotion, and through it maintain a passionate integrity among the other peoples of the earth.

The same intense conviction that Israel had been chosen for a special destiny runs through the next Books of the Old Testament, the narratives of Joshua and of Judges. In their long account of how Canaan was invaded and fought for, two influences are woven together in one inextricable pattern—a fierce conviction of religious purpose, and the primitive impulses of tribal warfare which could be let loose in the name of religion. So the story set forth in these Books must be read in the perspective of its far-off time. Here were men, out of the desert, fighting for what they believed was their God-appointed destiny. They had the courage that came from faith in something bigger than themselves, but they had also the untamed impulses that did not shrink from cruelty.

When the record of what they did came to be written down, it was natural that patriotic pride should glorify their exploits, and paint in vivid colors what was believed to have been the power of the Lord working through them to give them miraculous success.

Joshua was the leader now. This was what had come to him as divine command, "Arise, go over Jordan, you and all this people. Be strong and of good courage."

On the other side of Jordan stood the walled city of Jericho, and with the story of the taking of Jericho the saga of the conquest begins. Here, as later also in the Book, whatever were the first bare facts of fighting and of victory have been embroidered by the glamorous traditions that have made some of the events miraculous.

Before he was ready to launch his attack, Joshua sent two spies across the river. They got into Jericho, and to the house of a woman named Rahab. Rahab was a harlot, but that was not to prevent her from becoming regarded as a heroine in events that were to follow. Word got out that strangers were in her house, and there came a knocking at her door. She waited as long as she could to open it. Men sent from the authorities of Jericho confronted her, demanding to search her house. When the knocking began, she had hidden the spies under piles of flax on the roof. It was thin concealment, she well knew, and if she was to throw the searchers off, she had to act quickly. She pretended that the one thing she had been waiting for was to have help come. Yes, two suspicious looking men had tried to get into her house. But she had sent them away. They might have gone toward the river. If the men of Jericho ran, they could cut them off.

When the searchers had disappeared, she let the two spies out from their hiding place. That night they climbed out of a window, for her house was next to the city walls, and in the darkness made their way to the hills and at length back to Joshua's lines.

What was Rahab's motive? She said she had heard of all the victories Israel had been winning, and so it could have been that with a hard prudence she was buying favor on the winning side. But it could be believed also that in the woman's heart was some obscure but wistful intuition that Israel represented something better than the life she had known before; which would be the reason why Rahab's name is included in the Epistle to the Hebrews, in the great roll of those who were saved by faith. However that may be, Rahab said to the two spies whose lives she had saved, that as she had shielded them, so she wanted them to vow that she and her family would be shielded if fighting came to Jericho. They told her that she was to hang a red cord out of the window of her house—the window through which they had escaped —and if assault were made on the city, they promised that the house with that red cord should be protected.

When the spies had come back with such information as they had gathered about Jericho, Joshua was ready to launch the attack. Across the Jordan on a day when the water was low at the fords he sent the priests who carried the sacred ark, and all the ranks of the people followed after them and the armed men deployed on the fields of Jericho. "Now Jericho was shut up from within and without because of the people of Israel; none went out and none came in."

Then the narrative of the Book of Joshua goes on with the dramatic tradition of how the city fell:

"Joshua the son of Nun called the priests and said to them, 'Take up the ark of the covenant, and let seven priests bear seven trumpets of rams' horns before the ark of the Lord.' And he said to the people, 'Go forward; march around the city, and let the armed men pass on before the ark of the Lord.' And the armed men went before the priests who blew the trumpets, and the rear guard came after the ark, while the trumpets blew continually."

Thus the city was encircled, while the people of Jericho watched in silent apprehension from the walls, and there spread among them the fear which the spies had already found in Rahab.

The next day the ominous encirclement of the city was repeated. For six days that went on. Then on the seventh day Joshua ordered the attack. "So the people shouted, and the trumpets were blown. As soon as the people heard the sound of the trumpets, the people raised a great shout, and the wall fell down flat, so that the

people went up into the city, every man straight before him, and they took the city. Then they utterly destroyed the city, both men and women, young and old, oxen, sheep, and asses with the edge of the sword." Only Rahab and her family were sought out and left alive.

Thus the conquest of Canaan began, and was to continue through other grim events. It was assumed that dedication to the God of Israel meant extermination of Israel's enemies, and so the warfare was merciless. Discipline was merciless too. A man named Achan looted some of the wealth of Jericho that had been devoted to destruction, and Joshua had him stoned to death.

Other towns were taken, some by direct assault and some by stratagem. Some of the strands of developed narrative which are woven into the Book of Joshua make it appear that there was al-

Moses gives Pharaoh God's message, "Let my people go!"

Moses comes down from Sinai to find the people worshipping a golden calf.

most uninterrupted victory. But through that picture, as the instinctive patriotic bias shaped it, the less smooth reality emerges. The Israelites did seize parts of the land and hold it. In the rough hill country their man-to-man fighting could prevail. But on the plains they were outmatched. Among the Canaanites there were instruments of warfare which these invaders from the deserts did not have. So the men whom Joshua led "could not drive out the inhabitants of the plain, because they had chariots of iron."

Time went by, and Joshua was old. He said to the people, "I am about to go the way of all the earth." He reminded them all of the long story of the exodus, and of how they had been brought at length into the Promised Land. "Now therefore," he said, "fear the Lord, and serve him in sincerity and faithfulness; put away the gods which your fathers served beyond the River and in Egypt." Let the people make the dedication that he had tried to make. "As for me and my house," he said, "we will serve the Lord."

The people answered with the promise, "The Lord our God we will serve, and his voice we will obey."

But dedication to a purpose is more easily spoken than fulfilled. And as the later chroniclers looked back upon the history that followed the death of Joshua, and wrote of it in the Book of Judges, they saw that history as a continual inconsistency—idolatry and unfaithfulness, punishment and repentance, the appearance of some God-given deliverer and a period of salvation, then unfaithfulness and punishment again, and so, once more the fateful round.

The "Judges" in Israel were more than the word in modern terms would seem to mean. They were not men who sat quietly on some judicial seat and calmly settled points of law. They did speak with decisive action. When they told Israel what to do, they generally did so by way of weapons in their hands.

In one of the times of crisis it was a woman who was the rallying spirit, and a woman who brought the fighting to an end by an appalling act. Again the people had done "what was evil in the sight of the Lord; and the Lord sold them into the hand of Jabin, King of Canaan, who reigned in Hazor." His army was equipped with chariots, and its commander was Sisera.

In the hill country of Ephraim was a prophetess named Deborah, a woman whose flaming spirit could stir men to action. When she spoke, they listened. She summoned Barak, a tribal leader. "The Lord, the God of Israel, commands you," she said. "Go gather your men at Mount Tabor." Sisera with his chariots and troops would be converging there and Barak could meet him and defeat him.

So Barak with his fighting men moved toward what would be the battlefield. He took Deborah with him like a supernatural force. The seeming odds were all against him. The poorly armed Israelites could fight successfully in the hills, but this battle would be on the plain.

Yet the stars in their courses—as the exultant chant of victory would afterwards proclaim—fought for him. A great storm broke; the river Kishon, pouring down from the mountain, became a raging torrent. The flood engulfed the heavier equipment of the Canaanites. The wheels of their chariots bogged down and stalled, the struggling horses floundered, and the fighting men were caught in the wild confusion. The Canaanite army was cut to pieces, and its survivors scattered; among them, Sisera.

Alone and hunted, Sisera fled on foot until he came in sight of the tents of Heber, the Kenite, who was supposed to be a friend of the king of Canaan. Jael, Heber's wife, was at the tent door. "Come in, my lord," she said; "have no fear."

Sisera went in to the shelter of the tent, and Jael covered him with a robe. "Give me a little water to drink," he begged. Yes, she would give him better than that; so she brought him milk instead. And she would stand at the entrance to the tent, and if any pursuer came, she would tell him that the tent was empty.

Sisera, exhausted, fell asleep.

Then when Jael saw that Sisera was sleeping, she went and got a tent peg and a mallet. Stealthily she crept up by Sisera's head and drove the tent peg through his temple till the point of it went down into the ground.

Out beyond the tent she could see a man approaching. It was Barak, in pursuit of Sisera. She went out to meet him. "Come," she said, "I will show you the man that you are looking for." So he went into her tent, and there lay Sisera, dead, with the tent peg through his temple.

Always the passions of war have been able to take even the worst cruelties and exalt them into acts of patriotic courage. So the killing of Sisera by the woman in whose tent he had sought shelter was celebrated in what has been handed down through the centuries as the victory song of Deborah and of Barak.

> Awake, awake, Deborah!
>   Awake, awake, utter a song!
> Awake, Barak, lead away your captives
>   O son of Abinoam.
> The kings came, they fought,
>   then fought the kings of Canaan . . .
> From heaven fought the stars,
>   from their courses they fought against Sisera
> The torrent Kishon swept them away,
>   the onrushing torrent, the torrent of Kishon.
>   March on, my soul with might! . . .
> Most blessed of women be Jael,
>   the wife of Heber the Kenite
>   of tent-dwelling women most blessed,
> He asked water and she gave him milk,
>   she brought him curds in a lordly bowl.
> She put her hand to the tent peg
>   and her right hand to the workmen's mallet;
> She struck Sisera a blow.
>   she crushed his head,
>   she shattered and pierced his temple.
> He sank, he fell,
>   he lay still at her feet;
> at her feet he sank, he fell,
>   where he sank, there he fell dead.

And the fierce emotion out of which battle-songs and ballads grow did not stop with the death of Sisera. It went on with terrible dramatic vividness to imagine what it meant when the news of his death was brought to those who were waiting for his return.

Out of the window she peered,
  the mother of Sisera gazed through the lattice,
Why is his chariot so long in coming?
  Why tarry the hoofbeats of his chariots?
Her wisest ladies make answer,
  nay, she gives answer to herself.
Are they not finding and dividing the spoil?
  A maiden or two for every man;
Spoil of dyed stuffs for Sisera,
  spoil of dyed stuffs embroidered.
  two pieces of dyed work embroidered for my neck as spoil?
So perish all thine enemies, O Lord!
  But thy friends be like the sun as he rises in his might.

CHAPTER TWENTY-ONE

The Victory of Gideon's Three Hundred Men

THEN "the land had rest for forty years." But then comes again the recurrent refrain, "The people of Israel did what was evil in the sight of the Lord." This time "the Lord gave them into the hand of Midian."

The Midianites were one of the untamed Bedouin tribes that were continually raiding the settled land. From across the Jordan their camel-mounted marauders would appear, trampling the fields of the Israelites, carrying off the produce, driving the people before them to hide in caves in the hills. When they were gone, the land was left stripped and bare, so that "Israel was brought very low, and the people of Israel cried for help to the Lord."

This time deliverance was to come from a quarter almost as unexpected as had been true in the time of Deborah. There was a young man named Gideon, who was beating out wheat in a hidden wine press—to keep it, if he could, from the dreaded Midianites.

While he was working there one day under cover of an oak tree, Gideon looked up—and there before him was an angel.

"The Lord is with you," the angel said.

Great words to hear. But if the Lord was with him, how came it that Midianites overran the land? That is what Gideon made bold to ask. "Where are all the wonderful deeds which our fathers recounted to us? The Lord has cast us off," he said, "and given us into the hand of Midian."

But the Lord answered through the angel, "Go in this might of yours and deliver Israel from the hand of Midian." He would be the instrument that the Lord would use to answer Israel's cry.

To take the lead against the Midianites could be an appalling risk. Gideon shrank from it. He began to give his reasons why he was not the man for the Lord to choose—just as Moses had done when he was summoned to lead the people out of Egypt.

Gideon asked for one sign after another, and he was left with nothing more to say. The Spirit of the Lord had laid hold upon him, and the time had come to act.

The great sin to which the people of Israel were always being tempted was worship of the pagan gods—the local Baals of the Canaanites who were supposed to bring fertility to the land and reproduction to the flocks—and the worship of whom meant not moral integrity but license. Gideon thought the first thing he needed to do was to break down the nearby Baal altar—and that was what he did.

In the morning the men of the town discovered the broken altar. "Who has done this?" they demanded. When they learned that it was Gideon they told his father to bring him out for them to kill him.

But Gideon's father was not the sort of man who could be intimidated. They were taking up Baal's cause, were they? Well, if Baal was a god, let him contend for himself. His altar had been pulled down—and it could stay pulled down.

That ended the townspeople's threat to Gideon. Now came the more important matter of what to do about the Midianites.

Gideon sent messengers among the tribes, and men began to rally to him. But some of them seemed to Gideon to be a doubtful lot. For what had to be undertaken, he needed men about whom there could be no question. So there had to be a sifting out.

There would be rough work ahead, Gideon said. If any man had any fear about it, he had better drop out. The next morning more than two-thirds of the assembly had slipped away and gone home.

But Gideon had another test. He brought together all who were supposed now to be the fighting men and he ordered them forward as though he were leading them to where the Midianites would be found. Across their way there ran a brook of water and Gideon watched to see what his men would do when they came to it. Most of them—heedless of possible ambush from among the undergrowth along the banks—dropped down on their knees and plunged their faces into the stream to drink. But some of them did not. They kept on their feet, and only dipped up water in their hands and lapped it as they went on. "And the Lord said to Gideon, 'With the three hundred men that lapped I will deliver you, and give the Midianites into your hand. Let all the others go.' "

These men who had been winnowed out on the two tests proved to be enough, even when the Midianites "lay along the valley like locusts for multitude, and their camels were without number." At night Gideon sent his men through the darkness to surround the camp, while the Midianites had no knowledge that a single enemy was near. Each man had with him not only his sword and a trumpet; he had a torch that could leap into a fiery blaze, and a jar to cover it when the flame should first be lighted.

All round the camp in dead silence the three hundred men waited, poised for Gideon's signal. Then when the signal came, each man smashed the jar that covered his torch, blew his trumpet, and charged into the camp. Shocked out of sleep by the shattering noise, appalled by the closing ring of torches, the Midianites got to their feet too late. Gideon's swordsmen were among them, and in the blind confusion the Midianites began to strike at one another, and what was left of them were swept away in rout.

All the way to the Jordan River Gideon pursued those remnants from the defeat. His own men now were nearly spent. Gideon said to the townsmen of Succoth, "Give some loaves of bread to the men who follow me; for they are faint, and I am pursuing Zebah and Zalmunna, chiefs of Midian." But the people of Succoth refused. Gideon seemed to be prevailing now; but how did they know what might happen tomorrow or the day after? They had no intention of risking their necks by taking sides.

But they were to learn that there are times and choices when no men can be neutral. Gideon did not stop to argue. He went on until he had caught Zebah and Zalmunna. Then he went back to Succoth. He reminded the people of their refusal to give bread to his men until they should see who would be in power when the day was over. Well, they would find out now. And the narrative in the Book of Judges sets forth the climax with what seems sardonic brevity—"He took thorns of the wilderness and briers, and with them he taught the men of Succoth."

CHAPTER TWENTY-TWO

The Exploits of Jephthah, and of Samson

S OME OF Gideon's sons did not prove to be much of a credit to him. The worst of them, Abimelech, by treachery and cruelty made himself master of the stronghold of Shechem. Against him his brother Jotham told what came to be the famous parable of the trees—the trees that wanted a king, and were refused by the olive tree, the fig tree, and the vine, and at length had to settle for the worthless bramble. Abimelech was worthless and in the end Shechem had had enough of him, and in attacking the tower of another town he was struck by a great stone dropped by a woman from the parapet, and his skull was crushed.

Again, "the people of Israel did what was evil in the sight of the Lord." This time the Lord "sold them into the hand of the Philistines and into the hand of the Ammonites." With that name "the Philistines" there appears in Old Testament history for the first time the people who would have in the next years a fateful impact on the life of Israel. The Philistines were invaders from the Aegean islands and from Asia Minor who had invaded the eastern shore of the Mediterranean, north of Egypt, not long after 1200 B.C. They had attained a cultural development and an improvement in weapons that gave them formidable power; and as the influence of the Philistines reached out, the whole country that had been called Canaan received its name of Palestine.

Although both the Philistines on the west and the Ammonites from the country east of Jordan were threatening Israel, it was the Ammonites who struck first. This time the deliverer was Jephthah, and from the story of his victory two traditions stand out across the centuries as unforgettable.

One is the tragic tale of Jephthah's daughter. On his way out to meet the Ammonites, Jephthah made the reckless vow that if he should come back victorious, he would offer up in sacrifice whatever living thing first came out to meet him. When he did come

back, "Behold, his daughter came out to meet him with timbrels and with dances; she was his only child." For his vow's sake, he had to give her up to death, and so the legendary custom rose that "the daughters of Israel went year by year to lament the daughter of Jephthah the Gileadite four days in the year."

The other tradition linked with the name of Jephthah has come down in a word that has taken its enduring place in familiar language. When Jephthah was pressing his attack against the Ammonites, the tribe of Ephraim stood aside in angry jealousy; and at the end, Jephthah's men and the Ephraimites were embroiled with one another. The Ephraimites, defeated, tried to escape across the Jordan River; but Jephthah posted his men at all the fords. When any fugitive appeared, they said to him, "Are you an Ephraimite?" If he answered, "No," they said to him, "Then say 'Shibboleth,' and he said, 'Sibboleth,' for he could not pronounce it right. Then they seized him and slew him at the fords of the Jordan."

After Jephthah in the Book of Judges follows the story that has become the most vividly remembered drama of all during that turbulent time.

The Philistines now had reached out to dominate the land. In the tribe of Dan there was a man named Manoah whose wife had borne no child. She told her husband, "A man of God came to me and his countenance was like the countenance of the angel of God. He said to me, 'Behold, you shall conceive and bear a son.' " From his birth this son should be a Nazarite, which meant that he should be dedicated to God by special vows and by customs that he should never fail to keep.

So the son of Manoah and his wife was born, and they named him Samson.

When he was grown, he had a strength that no man could match, and none would dare to trifle with. The Philistines would find that out.

Samson fell in love with a Philistine girl. His father and mother tried to dissuade him. Why shouldn't he find someone among the daughters of Israel, they asked him, instead of seeking a wife among the uncircumcised Philistines? But when Samson had an idea in his head, he followed it with unreckoning abandon. His mighty body seemed to him so invincible that he did not often stop to use his mind.

So down to see the Philistine girl he went. On his path to Timnah, where she lived, he met a lion. Barehanded he killed it and jauntily went on his way. When he had finished his visit, he came back along the same path. There lay the body of the lion, which he had torn almost apart. A swarm of bees were building their honeycomb within it.

A little while after that, he took his father with him and went down to Timnah to be married. Young men of the town came to the wedding dinner. "Let me try you with a riddle," Samson said. If they could guess the riddle, he would pay what would be bet between them. If they could not guess it, they would pay him.

That suited them well enough. They did not think that Samson could give a riddle that one of them, or all of them together, could not figure out. So let him say what the riddle was.

"Here it is," said Samson:

"Out of the eater came something to eat
Out of the strong came something sweet."

The young Philistine men wrestled with that, and they could not get any answer out of it. But they were not going to lose the wager if by any hook or crook they could discover what Samson had hidden in the riddle. They went to Samson's bride. "Entice your husband to tell us what the riddle is," they said. Did she think that they had come to the wedding dinner just to be trapped into losing all their money? She would find out the answer for them, or they would set fire to her father's house.

So she went to Samson and began to cajole him. She cried, and she said, "You only hate me, you do not love me; you have put a riddle to my countrymen and you have not told me." He said he had not told it even to his father and his mother. But she cried again, and would not let go of him until at length he told her of the bees that had made honey in the body of the lion. She went and told her Philistine friends; and they came to Samson and said,

"What is sweeter than honey?
What is stronger than a lion?"

They had the answer to the riddle, and he would owe the bet. But he knew now where they had got the answer. "If you had not ploughed with my heifer," he said, "you would not have found out my riddle." They had seemed to get the best of him, and according to the wager, he owed them thirty linen garments, and thirty more fit to be worn to feasts. Well, they should see how he would pay them. In furious disgust, he went down to the Philistine town of Ashkelon, killed thirty Philistines there and brought their best clothes back to the men of Timnah.

CHAPTER TWENTY-THREE

Samson Is Betrayed by Delilah

N ow THE feud with the Philistines was on in deadly earnest. The next time Samson went down to Timnah he found that his father-in-law had given his wife to another man. Whatever he did now to any of the Philistines, Samson said, would be no more than they deserved. So at the time when the ripe wheat harvest was ready to be shocked in the fields, Samson went out and caught all the foxes he could find, tied lighted torches to their tails and let them loose into the standing grain, so that the wheat fields of the Philistines were set on fire and some of their olive orchards also.

Then the hatred which the Philistines had for Samson spread to wider fighting. Men from the Philistine towns got together and made a raid within the Israelite borders on the tribe of Judah. That was not the tribe to which Samson belonged, but Samson then was in their territory. They were in no mood to be mixed up in what they chose to think was only Samson's quarrel, and a great force of them came and surrounded him—too many for even Samson to deal with. They bound him with ropes, and handed him over to Philistines who came to take him.

Samson broke the ropes as though they were threads. He snatched up as a weapon the only thing he saw, the jawbone from the skeleton of a dead ass lying on the plain. With that he killed some of his would-be captors, and put the rest of them to flight. After that he went down into the Philistine city of Gaza and dared to spend the night there. When the report was spread that he was within the walls, the men of the town shut the gates so that he might not escape. But Samson tore the gates and the gate posts from their fastenings, slung them over his shoulders, and went off.

Still he would not let well enough alone, but walked into another peril more deadly than any that could be presented by the Philistine men.

He fell in love with another Philistine woman, whose name was Delilah.

The Philistine authorities knew too much now of Samson's power to think that they could capture him, unless somehow he should be betrayed. They went to Delilah and offered her a bribe. They would give her eleven hundred pieces of silver if she would entice Samson into disclosing the secret of his prodigious strength.

So Delilah let herself be made their tool. She begged him to tell her what it was that made him so strong. And what could ever happen that would make him not so strong?

He told her that if he were ever bound with seven fresh bowstrings, he would be as powerless as any other man. Moreover, he let her bind him. Philistine men who were hiding in the next room sprang in upon him; but Samson snapped the bow strings like so much tow touched by fire.

"You have mocked me!" cried Delilah. But though she had been shaken off once, she had a guile that like a serpent could coil again. She kept on trying to entice Samson to tell her the fatal truth.

Twice more he bantered her with pretended answers. If he were bound with new ropes; or if the locks of his hair were woven together by her fingers in a particular way; then his strength would go. But both times when she begged him to let her try, and the Philistines to whom she gave her signal tried to take him, he hurled them from him as before.

"How can you say 'I love you,' " she lamented, "when your heart is not with me? You have mocked me these three times, and you have not told me wherein your great strength lies." And when she pressed him hard day after day, he came to the point when it seemed to him that nothing could be worse than listening to her any longer. He would tell her the truth and be done with it.

"A razor has never touched my head," he said, "for I have been a Nazarite from my mother's womb. If I be shaved, then my strength will leave me, and I shall become weak, and be like any other man."

When Delilah saw that this time he had revealed the truth, she sent word to the Philistine authorities. "Come up this once, for he has told me all his mind." Then they came, bringing the money they had promised. She persuaded Samson to put his head upon her lap and go to sleep. While he was sleeping, she called a man who shaved all the long locks from his head.

Then she bent down and said to him, "The Philistines are upon you, Samson!"

Rousing up from his sleep he said, "I will go out as before, and shake myself free." But the vow that had given him his strength had been broken, and the Spirit of the Lord had left him. The Philistines seized him, gouged out his eyes, chained him and brought him into Gaza. There they harnessed him to a mill to grind their corn. The Samson who had towered over fighting men was now degraded into the blind captive who could be gazed upon and insulted by the crowd.

But the story was not yet complete. As time went on, Samson's hair grew out again and with it, his lost strength returned. The Philistines did not know that, and they took it for granted that they could still make cruel sport of him. On one of their feast days they had him brought out for exhibition. A boy led him by the hand, toward the temple where the gods of the Philistines were being honored. "Let me feel the pillars on which the house rests so that I may lean upon them," said Samson to the boy—the pillars of the temple in which the lords of the Philistines, and a great crowd of men and women, now were gathered.

"O Lord God," said Samson, "remember me I pray thee, and strengthen me, I pray thee, only this once, O God, that I may be avenged upon the Philistines for my two eyes!" He grasped the two middle pillars of the temple, leaning his weight upon them and straining with all his might. "Let me die with the Philistines," he gasped; and as he pulled the stones of the pillars loose, the house fell upon the people who were in it. His implacable warfare with the Philistines had come to that end described in the Book of Judges, "So the dead whom he slew at his death were more than those whom he had slain during his life."

CHAPTER TWENTY-FOUR

Samuel Listens to the Voice of the Lord

THE EVENTS described in the Book of Judges took place probably toward the end of the 12th century B.C. In the century
following, the assaults of the Philistines upon the Israelites were at
their worst. But a new and happier period in the history of Israel
was about to begin.

In the hill country of Ephraim there was a man named Elkanah,
whose wife was Hannah. Hannah grieved because she had no
child; and in her distress she went up to the shrine that was at
Shiloh and poured out her heart in prayer. She besought God to
give her a son; and if a son were given her, she would dedicate
him all his life long to the service of the Lord.

The old priest at the shrine, Eli, at first was impatient with her;
but when he learned what she was praying, he said to her, "Go in
peace, and the God of Israel grant your petition which you have
made to him."

Not long after that Hannah did have a son. She told Elkanah
of her vow; and when the little boy was old enough to leave his
mother, they took him to Shiloh, and Hannah said to Eli, "Oh,
my lord, I am the woman who was standing here in your presence,
praying to the Lord. For this child I prayed; and the Lord has
granted me my petition which I made to him. Therefore I have
lent him to the Lord; as long as he lives, he is lent to the Lord."

So the little boy Samuel lived in the temple at Shiloh with the
old priest, Eli. Eli depended on him more and more; for his own
sons had become a scandal in Israel because of their evil living,
and he had been lonely and sad.

One night in the temple, where the lamp was burning before the sacred ark, Samuel had lain down in his place to go to sleep. He heard a voice calling him, so he rose and ran to Eli. "Here I am," he said, "for you called me." "No," Eli said, he did not call.

Again Samuel heard the voice, and he went to Eli, and once more Eli said to him, "I did not call, my son; lie down again."

A third time Samuel heard the voice. This time Eli perceived that it was a different sort of message that was coming to the boy. He told Samuel that if the voice came again he was to answer, "Speak, Lord, for thy servant hears."

That was the way it happened. Samuel did answer as Eli had said; and as the boy grew, there were given to him revelations which the priest no longer had. When Samuel was a man, he became the first of those who would be listened to as God's prophets; for as a prophet, one who spoke for God, he would interpret the will of the Lord for Israel.

And Israel needed guidance and help. The Philistines were a continual threat. Fighting men of Israel came to Shiloh and took the ark from the shrine, to carry it before them into a pitched battle. But the Philistines defeated them, nevertheless; killed many of the Israelites, including both of Eli's sons; and captured the ark itself.

Eli was now very old, and also blind. He heard a great tumult in Shiloh, but he could not see that it was a crowd pressing around a messenger. Then the man came up to him and told him that he had fled from the battle.

"How did it go, my son?" the old man asked.

When he learned that both his sons were killed, and that the ark was taken by the Philistines, he fell from his seat, fatally breaking his neck. At the same time, the wife of one of Eli's sons gave birth in anguish to a child. The women who were with her tried to cheer her up. But she did not answer or take heed. Instead, she named the child Ichabod, meaning "The glory has departed from Israel!"

The Philistines carried the ark to their city of Ashdod, and set it up in triumph in the temple of their god. But then, in the Book

Samson betrayed by Delilah into the hands of the Philistines.

When the young David kept his father's sheep in the fields of Bethlehem.

King David.

The Queen of Sheba comes to see the magnificence of Solomon.

of Samuel there comes an account that is a curious mixture of grim fact and a groping search—half knowledge and half superstition—for an explanation. A plague broke out in Ashdod and the ark was sent away. It was sent to Gaza and then to Ekron. But wherever the ark went, the plague followed, and panic broke out in all the cities. Now, the one thing needed was to get rid of this ark that seemed to bring a curse—and in getting rid of it to placate somehow the avenging divine power that the ark was supposed to represent. So the Philistines put the ark on a cart and drove the oxen across the borders of Israel, and with it they sent votive images of mice, and of the tumors that had been on the bodies of men stricken by the plague, to be a kind of hoped-for magic. It may be that they were closer to reality than they knew, as tumors were one symptom of the Black Death which used to come with its recurrent terror here and there upon the earth. Also, the plague's contagion was spread by mice and rats.

The ark was carried from one place to another, but even in Israel men were fearful of it. A priest named Eleazar at Kiriath-jearim was supposed to be in charge of it. There for the time it rested, almost forgotten. The shrine of importance for Israel now was Mizpah, where Samuel had gone to live. He summoned all the people to come together there, and he offered sacrifices for their sins because many of them had been perverted into worshipping the heathen gods. And he set up an altar and called it *Ebenezer,* which meant, "This is witness that the Lord has helped us."

CHAPTER TWENTY-FIVE

Saul Is Made
King of Israel

N OW THERE pressed upon Samuel a demand for something the people believed they needed in order to resist the Philistines. The tribes were separate from one another and the people followed divided and sometimes jealous leadership. If they were to act together, there had to be someone who could command them all.

One day there came to Shiloh a young man of the tribe of Benjamin, named Saul. It might have seemed that his coming there that day was only an accident, for he was looking for some asses belonging to his father which had strayed away. But when Samuel saw him, he was sure that here was no accident. This was the man who was marked out for leadership in Israel.

He brought Saul to dinner at his house and seated him in the place of honor. He kept him there that night. The next morning, as Saul was about to leave, Samuel said to him, "Stop here for a while, that I may make known to you the word of God." Then he took a vial of oil and poured it on Saul's head, and he said, "Has not the Lord anointed you to be prince over his people Israel? And you shall reign over the people of the Lord and you will save them from their enemies round about."

The most courageous of the young men of Israel began to gather around Saul, for they saw in him the kind of leader that men could follow. He was strong and brave, and of noble height, for he was taller by a head than most of the men about him.

It was not long before a crisis came that summoned Saul to show what he could do. A raiding party from among the Ammonites attacked the town of Jabesh-Gilead, and the inhabitants knew that if the Ammonites took the town there would be savage cruelty. In desperation, they sent messengers to Saul, begging him to come to their aid.

When the word was brought to Saul, his anger flamed. He sent a peremptory summons through all the territory of Israel. He told the messengers from Jabesh-Gilead to go back and say, "Tomorrow, by the time the sun is hot, you shall have deliverance."

His deed was as good as his word. With the fighting men of Israel he went up to Jabesh-Gilead, fell upon the Ammonite camp in the early morning, and by noontime all the Ammonites who had not been killed were put to flight.

Now that their blood was up, the men who followed Saul turned to another score that they thought they would like to settle. On the day when Saul had first been presented by Samuel "to be prince over his people Israel," there were some who had had no use for him, and had treated him with contempt. The men who had just fought at Jabesh-Gilead remembered that. "Let's get hold of that crowd," they said, "and put them to death." But Saul would have none of it. "Today the Lord has wrought deliverance to Israel," he said, and there should be no acts of petty vengeance.

So it seemed that Saul's leadership was marked for greatness. He not only was formidable in battle; he could be magnaminous and self-controlled when other men would carry the fighting mood too far.

But the story that had an heroic beginning was to have a dark and tragic end. Over Saul's career there fell a shadow. Samuel became alienated from him. As the account unfolds in the First Book of Samuel, the justification for that is not wholly clear. After the victory at Jabesh-Gilead, Saul had gone out to another campaign, this time against the Philistines. At a moment of great peril Samuel was coming to offer a sacrifice and to pray to the Lord for help. When he did not come, at the time expected, Saul offered the sacrifice himself. To Samuel, when he did arrive, that seemed an act of arrogance. Saul was making himself not only king, but priest. "You have done foolishly," he said, "your kingdom shall not continue."

And what he said this day he said more sternly and irrevocably on a day that followed. Saul had gone out at Samuel's command to punish those ancient enemies of Israel, the Amalekites. In Samuel's conviction, and according to the fierce supposed justice which was part of the conscience of the time, that destruction must be complete. But Saul did not make it complete. He let his army bring back the Amalekite king and whatever they had taken as spoil from the Amalekite camp. And when Saul said to Samuel, "I have performed the commandment of the Lord," Samuel answered, "What then is this bleating of sheep in my ears, and the lowing of oxen which I hear?"

Saul tried to excuse himself. He had gone on the mission which had been assigned to him, and he had carried it out. It was "the people," he said, "who took the spoil."

"Stop!" said Samuel. "I will tell you what the Lord said to me this night. You have rejected the word of the Lord, and the Lord has rejected you from being king over Israel."

According to the code which to Saul's conscience as well as Samuel's was commanding, Saul had sinned. It may be also that Samuel had seen in Saul a growing wilfulness and pride of power more ominous than the two incidents might seem to show. At any rate, Samuel withdrew now from Saul the awesome blessing which he had once conferred upon him. He would choose another to take the place of Saul.

In the town of Bethlehem there was a man named Jesse, of the tribe of Judah, who had eight sons. Samuel went down to Bethlehem, and Jesse's eight sons were there before him. Samuel looked at Eliab the eldest, and he thought that this stalwart son of Jesse might be the Lord's anointed. But a voice within him said, "Do not look on his appearance or on the height of his stature, for the Lord sees not as man sees; man looks on the outward appearance, but the Lord looks on the heart."

Samuel then turned away from Eliab. He looked at Jesse's second son, but he said to Jesse, "Neither has the Lord chosen this one"; and as the others passed before him he said, "The Lord has not chosen these." At the end he asked, "Are all your sons here?"

"There remains only the youngest," Jesse answered. "He is keeping the sheep."

"Send and fetch him," said Samuel.

Then Jesse sent for the youngest son, and he came. He was ruddy and handsome and good to look upon. "Rise and anoint him," said the divine voice to Samuel. "This is he."

So Samuel took oil and anointed David there in the midst of his brothers. And it was written that "the Spirit of the Lord came mightily upon David from that day forward."

CHAPTER TWENTY-SIX

Saul and Jonathan, His Son

I N THE record as it has been handed down in the First Book of Samuel there is no indication that Saul knew at first of the anointing of David. He would learn of it later, and for that and other reasons David would become the prime object of his jealousy and hate. As yet that particular passion was not upon him. But already he was shadowed by a somber foreboding because of the breach with Samuel. His servants would come upon him sometimes in his tent and find him sunk in a depression so deep that he was like a man in a trance. The word spread that "The spirit of the Lord has departed from Saul, and an evil spirit torments him."

Now it was that David first appeared in the circle of Saul's awareness. The servants ventured to suggest to Saul that sometimes he might like to have someone come and play a harp before him—and they said they knew a person they could bring. Saul said to send for him. So they did send, and from the sheep fields by Bethlehem they brought David.

Now when the black moods came upon Saul, David would take his harp and play, and Saul would be refreshed. He came to love David and he kept David near him. Or it may be—for the account is not always clear—that David went back at first to tend his father's sheep, and came to Saul only when he was sent for from time to time.

There was another who began to love David with a deeper love than that of Saul. This was Saul's son, Jonathan. He was young, as David was; but already he had shown himself to have a courage and a daring that made him a hero among all fighting men. Saul had a fierce pride in him, but even toward Jonathan he could show a dangerous unreason which was the sign of a disordered mind.

In one of the recurrent clashes with the Philistines, Jonathan had performed an exploit which won the admiration of the whole army. With only his armor bearer beside him, he climbed up what was supposed to be an impassable path between rocky crags above which the Philistines were encamped, cut down the sentries, and caught the whole Philistine garrison in a panic of surprise, so that when Saul and the forces with him attacked from another direction, the entire Philistine army was put to rout.

At the beginning of the long pursuit which followed, Saul had ordered that no man should stop for any food, and had invoked a curse on anyone who did. Jonathan knew nothing of the curse, and passing a bee-tree, he saw there was honey dripping on the ground, and he took some. Men near him who had heard Saul's curse were appalled, but when they told Jonathan of it he brushed it off. How much better it would have been, he said, for the men with Saul to have eaten as they chose. They would have had more strength to follow the Philistines.

At the end of the day a priest was to offer a sacrifice so that they would receive a sign from the Lord as to what Saul should do next. But no sign came. Saul immediately concluded that something had brought divine displeasure. Someone might have sinned by violating the vow he had made that no one should touch food that day. He ordered that there should be a drawing of lots to see what the lots showed as to who it might have been.

The lots were drawn and they narrowed down to Saul and Jonathan—and then to Jonathan. "Tell me what you have done," said Saul.

"I tasted a little honey with the top of the staff that was in my hand," said Jonathan; and Saul answered, "God do so to me and more also. You shall surely die!"

But the men who had fought heard that with indignation. There was a stirring as of mutiny. "Shall Jonathan die, who has wrought this great victory in Israel?" they said. "Far from it!" So Jonathan was saved from execution, but Saul had shown how near to madness he could come.

CHAPTER TWENTY-SEVEN

David Fights
the Giant Goliath

THAT WAS one day of battle with the Philistines. Another and more famous encounter was to follow.

This time there was in the Philistine ranks a giant of a man, named Goliath. He would come out into the plain beneath the hill slope where the Philistine army was drawn up and dare any would-be champion of Israel to come out and fight him single-handed. He had a helmet of bronze on his head and greaves of bronze upon his legs, and a shield; a javelin was slung between his shoulders, he was girded with a sword, and in his right hand he had his spear, "the shaft of which was like a weaver's beam." From the plain he shouted to the ranks of Israel, "Why have you come out to draw up for battle? Am I not a Philistine, and are you not servants of Saul? Choose a man for yourselves, and let him come down to me. If he is able to fight with me and kill me, then we will be your servants. But if I prevail against him and kill him, then you shall be our servants and serve us. I defy the ranks of Israel this day; give me a man that we may fight together!"

It was not much wonder that the Israelites, looking at this huge man who was taller and stronger than any human being they had ever seen before, were dismayed and greatly afraid.

There was dead silence. No one took up the challenge. Not even Saul.

Day after day Goliath came out on the plain and hurled his insults, without response.

The older sons of Jesse were in Saul's army, and Jesse wanted to send them some bread and cheese. He called David from the sheep-fields and told him to go and find his brothers. And it happened that when he found them, it was by the battlefield and at the moment when Goliath stood on the plain and dared any man of Israel to come out and fight.

In excitement, David asked the men around him about Goliath. What had he said, and why had no one answered? What would happen if anyone said he would go out and face the Philistine? "Who is this uncircumcised Philistine," he asked, "that he should defy the armies of the living God?"

David's brothers overheard him and looked at him with angry contempt. What was he doing here anyway? He must have come down in idle curiosity, they said, instead of keeping to his business of taking care of the sheep.

But David was too concerned about Goliath to dispute with them. He asked more questions of the other men about Goliath, until word was brought to Saul, who sent for David. "There is no need for any man's heart to fail," said David. "Your servant will go and fight with this Philistine."

"You!" said Saul. "You are not able to go and fight with him! You are only a stripling and this Philistine ever since his youth has been a man of war."

But David was not deterred. He had not fought any Goliath, but he had met other dangers which had given him self-reliance— and reliance in something bigger than himself. "I used to keep sheep for my father," he said to Saul. "Sometimes a lion would come, or a bear, to take a lamb out of the flock. I would then go after them and kill them. The same will happen with this Philistine, because he has defied the armies of the living God." As for himself, said David, the Lord had delivered him before, and the Lord would deliver him again.

Saul looked at David; and then he took his own armor and began to gird David with it. "Go," he said, "and the Lord go with you."

But David was not used to armor. It only weighed him down. "I cannot go with this," he said.

What would he go with, then?

The sort of weapons that he had learned to use in the mountain pastures. He took his staff and shepherd's sling, picking up five smooth stones from the bed of the brook that flowed through the valley by the camp and thus he went out to meet Goliath.

The Philistine saw him coming. "Am I a dog," he shouted furiously, "that you come to me with sticks? Come on, then; and I will give your flesh to the vultures and the jackals." And the Philistine cursed David by his gods.

Yes, Goliath had his sword and spear and javelin, David admitted. But he had something more than that. "I come to you in the name of the Lord of hosts," he said. "This day the Lord will deliver you into my hand, and I will strike you down, that all the earth may know that there is a God in Israel, and that all this assembly may know that the Lord saves not with sword and spear; for the battle is the Lord's and he will give you into our hand."

Then as Goliath came on, David took one of the five stones from his shepherd's bag, fitted it in his sling, and with deadly

aim he let it go. It struck Goliath full in the middle of his fore-
head, going through flesh and bone. The Philistine pitched forward on his face and lay dead on the ground. Running to him and
standing over him, David took Goliath's own sword with which
he had been girded and cut off his head. And when the Philistines saw that their champion was dead, they fled.

CHAPTER TWENTY-EIGHT

Jonathan's Devotion
to David

FROM THAT day forward there developed for David a new friendship, and also a new hostility. Jonathan, Saul's son—Jonathan, the great-hearted and courageous—looked at this youth whose spirit was so like his own; and "the soul of Jonathan was knit to the soul of David, and Jonathan loved him as his own soul."

But what began to happen in the heart of Saul was very different. David had done what no man in his army had dared to do. David had won a great victory for all Israel. That was good, and Saul knew it. He kept David with him now and would not let him go back to his father's house. He set him over his fighting men, and all the people applauded.

Yes, but then what? This applause was beginning to drown out something more important. The acclaim for David was overwhelming, thereby obscuring Saul. In a great welcome for the army after their victory over the Philistines, the women came out from all the cities of Israel, singing and dancing, to meet King Saul. But what they sang was this:

"Saul has slain his thousands,
And David his ten thousands."

So *this* was what the people thought! David was the hero now, not Saul. David was given ten times more honor than the king. "What more can he have but the kingdom?" Saul asked himself. And from that day forward Saul began to eye David with an ugly suspicion that could be more deadly because at first it was concealed.

In the days when Goliath was challenging the men of Israel great promises had been made toward whatever man would go to meet him. He should be richly rewarded, even to being given one of Saul's daughters for his wife. Saul remembered that. His daughter Michal fell in love with David, and now Saul thought of a way in which she could be made a snare. He told David that he could have Michal only if he brought as a wedding dowry the evidence of a hundred dead Philistines whom he was to kill in battle. He was confident that David would be killed instead, and thus he would be rid of his rival once and for all. But David went out to do battle and killed more than a hundred of the enemy. Sullenly Saul gave him Michal, but now he feared David more than ever.

Meanwhile, Jonathan's devotion had no bounds. He gave David his own robe and his armor, including his sword and his bow. But he knew now how his father felt. For one day when David had been playing the harp before Saul, Saul with sudden savage impulse had hurled his javelin at David, trying to pin him to the wall.

Jonathan tried to change his father's spirit. He said to Saul one day that he ought not to do wrong to David. "He has not sinned against you," he said; "he has been of good service. He took his life in his hand and he slew the Philistine. The Lord wrought a great victory for Israel. You saw that, and rejoiced; why then will you sin against innocent blood by killing David without cause?"

The conscience which was never quite buried beneath the fierce malignity that sometimes took possession of Saul was touched. He said to Jonathan "As the Lord lives, David shall not be put to death."

So for a while David went in and out of Saul's presence as before. But not for long. Again one day in a sudden passion Saul hurled a javelin at him. When the javelin missed its aim and David escaped, Saul sent men to his house to watch whether he came back there and to kill him in the morning. But Michal, his wife, let him down through a window while Saul's men were watching the door. David then got away to Ramah to find Samuel and to tell him all that Saul had done.

David made contact also with Jonathan. "What have I done?" he said. "What is my guilt before your father that he seeks my life?" Jonathan still could not believe that Saul's real purpose was as murderous as David thought. But David said to him, "As the Lord lives and as your soul lives, there is only a step between me and death."

Jonathan answered, "Whatever you say I will do for you."

Therefore it was arranged that Jonathan would find out Saul's mind, and let David know. Because it was too uncertain yet whether David might dare to come where Saul was, they agreed upon a signal.

It was the time of the new moon, and at Saul's court it was part of the required ceremony that all who were connected with the king should be present at his table. Saul sat at his accustomed place, and Jonathan sat opposite him. Saul looked up and saw that David's place was empty. The first day he said nothing, but the second day he demanded, "Why has not the son of Jesse come to the meal, either yesterday or today?"

Jonathan replied as he and David had agreed. David had asked that Saul be told that he had gone to Bethlehem to observe a yearly sacrifice with his family, and therefore begged permission of Saul to be absent. So Jonathan said, and he ended; "This is the reason why he has not come to the king's table."

Here was the test of Saul's mood. In better times he would readily have accepted David's excuse. But now he burst into furious anger, not only against David but against Jonathan also. "You son of a perverse and rebellious woman!" he shouted, "do I not know that you have chosen the son of Jesse to your own shame? For as long as the son of Jesse lives upon the earth, neither you nor your kingdom shall be established. Therefore send and bring him here, for he shall surely die!"

"Why should he be put to death? What has he done?" asked Jonathan. At which Saul was so enraged that he cast his spear at Jonathan, and Jonathan rose from his place at the table in fierce anger and in grief for David.

The next morning he gave David the sign that had been worked out between them. It was not safe for David to come where the

servants of Saul could see him, and so he was to watch in concealment, at a distance. Then Jonathan went out into a wide field to
shoot arrows at a target, and with him a boy to pick up the arrows
that he shot. "The arrow is beyond you," he called out to the boy
who was following. It was the signal to David that he was in mortal
danger and must get away.

Then Jonathan sent the boy home not knowing that there had
been any signal or that David was near. And Jonathan himself
went out to where David was hidden and they embraced one another and wept. Whatever Saul might try to do, nothing could
touch the loyalty of Jonathan. "We have sworn both of us in the
name of the Lord," he said, "that 'the Lord shall be between me
and you, and between my descendants and your descendants, forever.' "

CHAPTER TWENTY-NINE

Saul's Hatred of David, and His Death

Now SAUL had committed himself to a vengeful pursuit of David which he would never abandon—even though he might have rare spasms of remorse. The hatred that he had for David grew into a mania that could involve in its consequences anyone who seemed to be on David's side. Fleeing from Saul, David and a few men with him had gone to a shrine ministered to by a priest named Ahimelech. Ahimelech had fed him and his men with some of the hallowed bread. Also at that shrine was the sword of Goliath the Philistine; and David, who was weaponless, had asked to have it. Ahimelech did give him what he asked; but not long afterward came Saul and his armed men with him. "Why have you conspired against me, you and the son of Jesse?" Saul demanded of Ahimelech; but Ahimelech was amazed. "Who among all your servants is so faithful as David?" he asked. If Saul had anything against David, he had never heard of it, either much or little.

But Saul ordered Ahimelech and the other priests at the shrine to be slain. They were then cut down by the swords of Saul's escorting guardsmen.

Like a hunted thing, David had to find harborage wherever he could. For a while he even went into the country of the Philistines, where he pretended that he was mad. Then with a group of men who had gathered around him he retreated into a barren tract called the Wildgoats' Rocks. Close on his heels came Saul.

One night Saul lay down to sleep in a cave. In the deeper recess of that same cave, unknown to Saul, was David. In the darkness

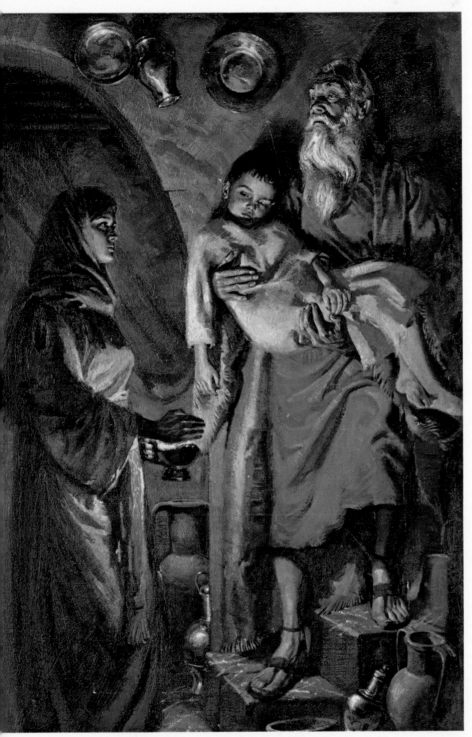

Elijah brings back to life the widow's son.

After the wind and the earthquake, Elijah hears the quiet voice of God.

he could have killed Saul, and no man would have known it. But he would not touch him.

A second time Saul's life was in his hands. From a hillside David saw the tents of his pursuers, and he knew that Saul was there. Who would go down with him to Saul's camp? One of his men named Abishai volunteered to go. So the two of them crept near under cover of the dark.

There lay Saul himself, his spear stuck into the ground beside him. Around him, asleep, lay Abner, the captain of Saul's guard, and the rest of his men.

"God has delivered your enemy into your hand," Abishai whispered. "Let me pin him to the earth with one stroke of the spear, and I will not strike him twice!"

But David would not hear of it. God forbid, he said, that he should strike the Lord's anointed.

He took Saul's spear and a jar of water that was by his head, and he and Abishai went out of the camp as noiselessly as they had come. Nor did Saul or any of the men lying near him wake.

David went to a hill slope at a distance. Through the darkness he called aloud to Abner. And again. Then—"Will you not answer, Abner?"

Rousing himself heavily, Abner answered, "Who are you that calls to the king?"

"What sort of a man are you," said David, "you who were supposed to keep watch over your lord, the king? Look and see where the king's spear is, and the jar of water that was by his head."

Saul also was awake now. When he heard David's voice and realized what had happened, for a sudden moment his old and better self broke through. "Is this your voice, my son David?" he said.

"Yes, it is my voice, my lord, O king," David answered. "Why does my lord pursue after his servant? What guilt is on my hands, that the king of Israel has come out to seek my life?"

Then, as though with bitter wrestling of his soul, Saul cried out. "I have done wrong! Return, my son David, for I will no more do you harm. I have played the fool, and have erred exceedingly."

So in Saul's words there was reconciliation. But David knew better than to think that Saul's dangerous instability could be trusted again. Saul's spirit had been so poisoned by the jealousy and angry pride which had possessed him that his hostility had reached the point of no return. Ahead of him now lay only darkness of mind, and oncoming doom.

Samuel had died, and that gave Saul a strange sense of loneliness. Even though Samuel had turned against him, still Saul felt that Samuel was a link between him and the help of the Lord which in the old days he had relied on. There was a woman who as a medium was reputed to be able to call up the spirits from the dead; and though Saul himself had once made a decree banishing all mediums and pretenders to magic, he now sought out this woman, who was called the Witch of Endor. He went by night, and in disguise, so that she would not know him.

"Bring up for me," he said, "the one I shall name to you."

Didn't he know, the woman asked, that Saul had prohibited all mediums and wizards in his kingdom? What was he trying to do? Lay a trap for her?

But he swore to her that no punishment should come to her for anything she did.

"Whom shall I bring up for you?" she asked. And he answered, "Bring up Samuel."

"You are Saul!" the woman screamed. "Why have you deceived me?"

But Saul convinced her that she need not be afraid; and when she had gone into her trance, he asked her, "What do you see?"

"I see a god coming up out of the earth," she answered. And when Saul asked "What is his appearance?" she continued. "An old man is coming up, and he is wrapped in a robe."

"Why have you disturbed me by bringing me up?" the shade of Samuel demanded. And Saul, with his face bowed to the earth, exclaimed, "I am in great distress; for the Philistines are warring against me, and God has turned away from me and answers me no more, either by prophets or by dreams. Therefore I have summoned you to tell me what I shall do."

But there was no comfort in Samuel's answer. "Why then do you ask me," he said, "since the Lord has turned from you and become your enemy. The Lord has done to you as he spoke by me; for the Lord has torn the kingdom out of your hand, and given it to your neighbor, David." And the words went on to a fateful climax. Israel would be delivered into the hands of the Philistines; and tomorrow Saul and his sons would be with Samuel in the realm of the dead.

Now there was nothing to wait for but the end.

On a field in the shadow of Mount Gilboa the army of the Philistines clashed with the army of Saul. With Saul were his sons, including the great-hearted Jonathan. Through all the bitter happenings that had gone from bad to worse, Jonathan had kept his double loyalty; never wavering in his devotion to David, yet never forsaking his father, even when his father had threatened his own life. Now in the press of the battle Jonathan was killed, and an arrow wounded Saul. Alone, except for his armor-bearer, Saul looked and saw that the ranks of his army were broken and about to be put to rout. "Draw your sword and thrust it through me," Saul said to his armor-bearer; but the armor-bearer was afraid and would not.

Then came the final act that summed up the tragedy of Saul's life. He took his sword and fell upon it, thereby killing himself. Through his great power, no longer used in the Lord's service, but turned in by pride and passion upon himself, he had killed what had once been the greatness of his soul.

Yet the story of Saul does not conclude in ugliness. It is lifted to its climax in one of the noblest passages in the Old Testament. When David heard that Saul and Jonathan were slain, he lamented for them both:

> "Thy glory, O Israel, is slain upon thy high places!
>> How are the mighty fallen!
> Tell it not in Gath,
>> publish it not in the streets of Ashkelon
>> lest the daughters of the Philistines rejoice
>> lest the daughters of the uncircumcised exult . . .
>
> Saul and Jonathan, beloved and lovely!
>> In life and in death they were not divided;
> they were swifter than eagles,
>> they were stronger than lions
> Ye daughters of Israel, weep over Saul . . .
>
> Jonathan lies slain upon thy high places—
>> I am distressed for you, my brother Jonathan.
> very pleasant have you been to me;
>> your love to me was wonderful,
>> passing the love of women.
> How are the mighty fallen,
> and the weapons of war perished!"

CHAPTER THIRTY

David Succeeds
to the Kingship

W ITH SAUL, Jonathan and Samuel dead leadership in Israel
would belong to the one who would be strong enough to
take it.

David had shown that he was the sort of man around whom
other man would rally. At the time when Saul was pursuing him,
compelling him to be a fugitive, a considerable number, who for
one reason or another had become outlaws, were attracted to him.
Like a primal Robin Hood, he and his band were no threat to the
common people, but the prosperous and arrogant could have
reason to be afraid.

In the region of Carmel there was a man named Nabal who
was rich in flocks and herds. While his sheep were in the upland
pastures David's men in the hills had done no violence to the
shepherds. At the time of sheep-shearing, David sent some of his
men to Nabal to remind him that it would be a good thing for
him to show his thanks. Now Nabal's wife, whose name was
Abigail, was both beautiful and of a quick understanding, but
Nabal was churlish and stupid.

He did not see the danger of rousing the hot blood of men
who were already outlaws. "There are plenty of servants now-
adays," he said, "who break away from their masters." Why should
he take good bread and meat that he could use and give it to men
he had never heard of? David's messengers would get nothing, so
far as he was concerned.

When Abigail learned of Nabal's answer, she knew the folly
of it. Without telling Nabal, she had her servants load some
asses with five dressed sheep and bread, raisins and figs. She then

set out to find David. She was just in time, for David, furious at Nabal's insulting message, was coming down from the hills with his armed men to settle accounts with Nabal. "It has all been in vain," he said, "that I have guarded this fellow's possessions out in the wilderness. He has paid back good with evil. May God deal with me if I have failed to deal with him by morning."

When Abigail saw David coming, she got down from the ass she was riding and bowed to the ground before David. She told him that she had not known at first about his messengers who had come to Nabal, and so she had no part in Nabal's answer. She had no excuse for his ill nature. But she begged David now to accept the presents she had brought, and to stay his hand from any violence.

As David looked at her, he had a sudden change of heart. Except for her, he admitted, he would have carried out his vengeance on Nabal and on whatever belonged to him. But her plea had saved him from what might have been blood guilt. He could thank God for that, and she could go home in peace.

When she did go home she found Nabal at a feast, drunk. She said nothing to him that night, but the next morning she told him all that had happened. Then—what with his drinking, the jolt to his greed in what Abigail had given away and the shock of knowing how deadly the anger of David might have been—he had a stroke, and not many days after that he died. When David learned that Nabal was dead, he married Abigail.

Now that Saul had fallen in the battle at Mount Gilboa and his kingship was at an end, there was nothing to keep David as an outlaw any longer. Instead the way was open toward the leadership in Israel for which Samuel had destined him. Others were quick to see that, and began to do what they thought would win them David's favor.

On the third day after the battle, there appeared a man in torn, dishevelled clothes. "Where do you come from?" David asked. "I have escaped from the camp of Israel," he answered; and he told David of the rout of the Israelite army and of how Saul and Jonathan had fallen.

What did he himself know about it, David asked? And the man made up the sort of lie that he imagined would win reward.

He said that there on the battlefield he saw Saul leaning on his spear, with the chariots and horsemen of the Philistines closing in upon him. Saul had asked him to kill him, and that is what he had done. "And I took the crown that was on his head, and the armlet that was on his arm, and I have brought them here."

He had supposed that David would gloat over the death of the king who had pursued him. But with David there were some loyalties to which he could endure no treachery. Instead of rewarding the man who had brought him the trophies from the dead Saul, he turned upon him in outraged anger. "How is it you were not afraid to lift your hand against the Lord's anointed?" he demanded. "Your blood be upon your own head." And he ordered the men about him to take this man and kill him.

In the days that followed, David became involved in what would prove sometimes a cruel struggle for the kingship, which Saul's death had left vacant; but the cruelty was not David's. He went to Hebron in the territory of his own tribe of Judah, and there the men of Judah anointed him as king. At the same time, in the territory of Saul's tribe, Abner, who had been the commander of Saul's army, took Ishbosheth, one of Saul's sons, and set him up as king. Then there was war between the two factions, until Abner was treacherously killed by Joab who thought he was serving David; and Ishbosheth was stabbed to death by two men who broke in upon him as he lay in bed. Both times David was bitterly ashamed. He mourned and fasted for the killing of Abner; and the two men who had stabbed Ishbosheth were executed as had been the man who claimed that he had killed Saul.

Nearly all of Saul's descendants were dead, but one at least was left. This was Mephibosheth, a son of the beloved Jonathan. He was a cripple, lame in both feet. David sent for him, and from that time forward he ate at David's table and was treated as one of David's own sons.

The resistance to David came to an end and he was acknowledged as king over all Israel. Under him the borders of Israel were widened, and, most important, the stronghold of Jerusalem was taken and made the capital of the kingdom. David saw that the sacred ark was brought there from Kiriath-jearim, and installed in what would be the people's holiest shrine.

CHAPTER THIRTY-ONE

David's Sin with Bathsheba

THERE WERE qualities in David which seemed to fulfill what old Samuel was looking for when he sought to anoint one who would be a king "after God's own heart." The clearest tribute to David's manhood was in the kind of devotion he could win. Remembered, and written in the Second Book of Samuel, was what happened in one of the encounters between Israel and the Philistines. The two armies were encamped opposite each other, and behind the Philistine camp was Bethlehem. As David gazed in that direction, the memories of his boyhood flooded over him. "Oh that I had a drink of the water from the well that is by the gate of Bethlehem!" he said. Three of his men overheard him as he breathed that wish. That night they risked their lives to go through the Philistine lines to bring David water from the Bethlehem well. The water they brought him he took in his hands then and lifted up as a holy thing. He poured out part of it as a sacrifice to the Lord, and as a gesture of honor to the men who had hazarded so much for him.

But the same David who could be magnanimous and noble had also his intensely human faults which would blot his record and leave their mark upon his soul. The worst of these was in what he did to a man in his army named Uriah.

Late one day David was walking on the flat roof of his house, and from the roof he saw a woman bathing. She was beautiful, and David desired to have her. When he inquired about her, he learned that she was Uriah's wife. Notwithstanding that, he brought her to his house; and not long afterward Bathsheba told him that she was with child.

To cover up what he had done, David sent orders to Joab, the commander of his army, that Uriah should be given leave and that he should report to him. When Uriah came, David pretended that what he wanted was to learn directly through Uriah of all that was going on in the army; and then Uriah should go home and have a rest and spend the days and nights with his wife. But Uriah would not listen. He said that his place was with the army, and back to the army he would go.

Caught more deeply in the consequences of his wrongdoing, David now turned to the one final way by which Uriah would never know what had happened to his wife. He would get rid of Uriah altogether. So he sent word to Joab that during the next battle Uriah should be put in the front rank, at the point in the battle where the fewest were likely to survive. Joab did put Uriah there, and when the fighting was over, he sent a message to David to tell him that Uriah had been killed.

Then David took Bathsheba for his wife; and not long afterward, their child was born.

But the evil he had tried to keep in the dark was to be brought to light. There was a man of God named Nathan, and one day he confronted David. He had something to tell the king. David listened, thinking that Nathan had some need of his own, or some plea on behalf of others, for which the king's justice was besought.

"There were two men in a certain city," Nathan began; "the one rich and the other poor. The rich man had very many flocks and herds, but the poor man had nothing but one little ewe lamb, which he had bought. And he brought it up, and it grew up with him and with his children; it used to eat of his morsel, and drink from his cup, and lie in his bosom, and it was like a daughter to him. Now there came a traveler to the rich man, and he was unwilling to take one of his own flock or herd to prepare for the wayfarer who had come to him, but he took the poor man's lamb, and prepared it for the man who had come to him."

Nathan stopped. Before his final words were spoken, David's anger flared. So here was something that had happened in his

kingdom—a cruel and callous thing! "As the Lord lives," said David, "the man who has done this deserves to die, because he did this thing, and because he had no pity!"

Then Nathan, looking full into David's face, spoke his devastating judgment—"*You* are the man!"

Shocked into silence, David listened as Nathan went on to lay bare his sin with Bathsheba and the killing of Uriah which he had contrived. Punishment for it should come to him, and also fall on his descendants. What David had done, he had done secretly; but the retribution from the Lord, said Nathan, would be before all Israel and as clear as the light of the sun.

David had no defense. Nathan in his parable had thrown David off his guard, and reached through to David's decent self in the light of which he stood condemned. "I have sinned against the Lord," he said.

Then David went down to his house and mourned and fasted. The child that had been born to Bathsheba had fallen ill. On the seventh day it died.

CHAPTER THIRTY-TWO

The Rebellion and Death of Absalom

D AVID HAD other children, and the stain of David's own sins would appear again in them.

One of David's sons, Amnon, violated his own sister, Tamar. When Absalom, another son, heard from Tamar what Amnon, their brother, had done, he determined to avenge her. He waited for an occasion when he was giving a feast at his house, and Amnon was there. Then Absalom told his servants to watch when Amnon had drunk his fill of wine. Then they were to set upon him and kill him. And that was what his servants did.

Absalom fled and David decreed that he should be banished from the kingdom. But after three years, Joab contrived to get David to relent. Absalom was allowed to come to Jerusalem to live in a house of his own. For two more years David would not see his face; but again Joab interceded and at length David received Absalom once more as his son.

Now Absalom was very handsome, and he could be full of charm. He got himself a chariot and horses and fifty men to run before him. He would rise early in the morning and go out to the city gate where the people congregated. If he learned of any man who had a complaint that he wanted to bring before the king, Absalom would call him and ask him where his home was and what his complaint might be. When the man told him that he was from such and such a tribe, Absalom would ask him more about what he wanted and tell him that his claim was sound and right. "But there is no one appointed by the king to hear you," he said. And then, as though he were moved by generous sympathy, he

sighed, "Oh that I were judge in the land! Then every man with a
suit or cause might come to me, and I would give him justice."

Moreover, he did not stand on what might have been supposed
to be his dignity as the king's son. If any man bowed down
humbly before him, Absalom would put out his hand and lift him
up and embrace him. So, before David's eyes were opened to what
was happening, Absalom stole the hearts of the men of Israel.

Then, when Absalom considered that the time was ripe, he
told his father that he wanted to go to Hebron to fulfill a vow.
David said to him, "Go in peace." However, the reason for
Absalom going to Hebron was far from fulfilling a vow. When he
arrived in Hebron, he sent messengers through all the tribes of
Israel saying, "As soon as you hear the sound of the trumpet,
then say 'Absalom is king at Hebron!' "

The conspiracy was well planned, and it spread through Israel
like a flame. The tidings came to David, "The hearts of the men
of Israel have gone after Absalom." David himself was in peril
now. With the servants and men-at-arms who were still loyal to
him he abandoned Jerusalem in flight from Absalom.

Zadok the priest went with him, bearing the ark. But David
told him to return with the ark into Jerusalem. "If I find favor in
the eyes of the Lord," he said, "he will bring me back to see the
ark and its shrine again. But if he says, 'I have no pleasure in
you,' behold here I am. Let him do to me what seems good to
him." He sent Abiathar also with Zadok into the city, and also
Hushai, another man of whose loyalty he was sure. These men
would be there when Absalom came, and they would be able to
get word to David as to what might happen then.

Absalom did enter the city and immediately began to take
counsel as to which way David had gone and as to how the king
and the men who were with him could be overtaken and made
captive. One of the first persons he encountered in Jerusalem was
Hushai, and Hushai began immediately to play his dangerous
part as David's man who would pretend now to have gone over to
Absalom. "Long live the king!" he said. When Absalom began to
demand of Hushai what sort of loyalty was this of his and why he
had not gone with David, Hushai answered that the men of Israel

had chosen Absalom, and "As I have served your father, so will I serve you."

Absalom's first impulse was to go immediately in pursuit of David. But he made the mistake of turning to Hushai and asking what he thought. Hushai said that quick pursuit would be a mortal risk. All Israel knew the valor of David, he said, and of the men who would fight at his side. No hasty attack could succeed against them. What Absalom ought to do was to wait until he had gathered men from everywhere in Israel—enough men so as not to be defeated when they came face to face with David.

Absalom listened. Then, to his own undoing, he let himself believe that what Hushai said was true. He would wait until he had a stronger force. But in the meantime David and the men who guarded him, who at first were almost defenseless, had reached the Jordan River, and crossed to the other side.

As soon as he was ready, Absalom set his forces in motion. He rode with arrogant assurance, and with no restraint of conscience in going against his father. But there was one weakness in his support which would have fatal consequences. Joab, who had been the commander of David's army, had also been the one who in the early days had gone farthest in advancing the interests of Absalom. Whether Joab had been ready now to come on Absalom's side is not plain in the narrative, but what is certain is that Absalom chose not Joab but another man for the post of command. Now, when Absalom should encounter Joab next, he would be encountering the hidden anger of a proud and passionate man who felt himself to have been insulted.

Absalom crossed the Jordan, and battle was begun in the forest of Ephraim. After the first shock of Absalom's rebellion, Israel woke to its real loyalty, and more men rallied to David's standard. David's heart was heavy, not so much because of his own danger as because the man from whom that danger came was his own son. In spite of everything, he still loved Absalom. "Deal gently with Absalom" was the order he gave as the battle began.

But the fighting turned into a confused struggle in the forest. Absalom, riding with his head bent beneath the branches of a great oak, had his long thick hair caught by part of a branch and was jerked violently from his saddle. As he hung there stunned, a man who saw him ran and told Joab, "I saw Absalom hanging in an oak!"

"What, you saw him?" Joab exclaimed. "Why didn't you strike him to the ground?"

The man was horrified. "Even if I felt in my hand the weight of a thousand pieces of silver, I would not lift my hand against the king's son," he said.

"I will not waste time like this with you," the angry Joab answered. He took three darts in his hand, and thrust them into the heart of Absalom, while he was still alive in the oak.

But how should the tidings now be brought to David?

A man named Ahimaaz asked Joab to let him run and carry the word to the king that "the Lord has delivered him from the power of his enemies." But Joab held him back, and sent another messenger, called the Cushite.

Ahimaaz again begged Joab to let him go.

"Why do you want to go?" Joab demanded. Absalom was dead, and that seemed good enough news to the men who had killed him; but it would be different news to his father David. Did Ahimaaz imagine that he would get a reward from David for what he would run to tell?

But Ahimaaz pleaded, "Come what may, I will run." So Joab let him go.

Then Ahimaaz outran the Cushite and came within sight of the town where David was waiting. A watchman on the wall saw him approaching. He called out to David that a messenger was coming.

A moment later he saw the Cushite. "I see another man running," he cried to David; and then he said, "I think the running of the foremost is like the running of Ahimaaz, the son of Zadok."

"He is a good man," said David. "He is coming with good tidings."

"All is well," Ahimaaz panted. And bowing to the earth before the king he said, "Blessed be the Lord your God, who has delivered up the men who raised their hand against my lord the king."

But there was one thing only that David's heart desired first to know. "Absalom," he said, "is it well with Absalom?"

Ahimaaz looked at David, and now he knew he could not bring himself to tell the fatal truth. "When Joab sent your servant, I saw a great tumult," he answered; "but I do not know what it was."

"Turn aside," said David, "and stand here."

Then came the Cushite. "Good tidings for my lord the king!" he cried. "The Lord has delivered you today from the power of all who rose up against you."

Again from David broke the one urgent question. "Is it well with Absalom?"

Heedlessly the Cushite went on with what he thought were the exultant tidings. "May the enemies of my lord the king, and all who rise up against you for evil, be like that young man."

Then David understood. Like a stricken soul he made his way to his room over the gate, and as he went he cried, "O my son Absalom, my son, my son Absalom! Would God I had died instead of you. O Absalom, my son, my son!"

CHAPTER THIRTY-THREE

David Dies, and Solomon Is King

N OW THAT the rebellion which had centered in Absalom was broken, David went back to Jerusalem to resume his kingship. He would not permit any act of vengeance upon those who had turned against him, neither upon those who had fought in Absalom's ranks, nor upon such a one as the man Shimei who had come out on a hillside and cursed him on the day when he had been driven from Jerusalem.

Not many more years were left of David's kingship. Finally the day came when he said to his son Solomon, "I go the way of all the earth." When he died he had reigned as king for seven years in Hebron where the men of the tribe of Judah had anointed him, and for thirty-three years more as king of all Israel. And though he died, there had been more to him than that which goes "the way of all the earth." In the thought of Israel he was idealized. He became endeared because of his humanness. He was close to the understanding of ordinary men in that he committed grave sins of the flesh, but he was brave and loyal, and he was capable also of tenderness and of quick compassion. Above all, he was a man who had a conscience, and because he saw his own life not in terms of his world alone but in the dimensions of the judgments of God, he could be moved by great emotions— of prayer and of thankfulness, of trust and yet of humility, of desire for goodness and yet of recognition of his actual guilt. As the laws of Israel had been attributed to Moses, so its poetry was attributed to David. His name was afterwards attached to most of what was gathered into the Book of Psalms. It is evident now that many, if not all of the psalms that bear his name could not have been written by him, or in his time. But the fact that they were believed to be his is a witness to the extent to which his life had been a mirror of what the soul of Israel was seeking. It was seeking what the special cry of the fifty-first psalm expresses, and what it could well be believed that the lips of David himself had uttered:

> Have mercy upon me, O God,
> according to thy great goodness,
> According to the multitude of thy mercies
> blot out my transgressions.
> Wash me thoroughly from my iniquity,
> and cleanse me from my sin.
> Create in me a clean heart, O God,
> and put a new and right spirit within me.
> Cast me not away from thy presence,
> and take not thy holy Spirit from me.
> The sacrifice of God is a troubled spirit,
> a broken and contrite heart, O God,
> thou wilt not despise.

When David died, his son Solomon succeeded him. There was an ugly period of violence as Solomon was establishing his power. Adonijah, another son of David's and like his brother Absalom a very handsome man, had been the first claimant to the kingship, but the influences backing Solomon prevailed. Before long, Solomon had Adonijah put to death; and put to death also was Joab, the man who had killed—and sometimes treacherously— many other men.

It was in the year 961 B.C. that Solomon became king. The conditions were such that his reign would become famous, both for what actually happened and also because of legendary traditions that enlarged the history. David had widened and strengthened the borders of Israel, both as regards the Philistines on the side toward the sea, and as regards the marauding tribes of the deserts to the east. The lands of Israel included and controlled the highroads that led from Egypt in the south to Damascus in the north, and on to the great empires in the Mesopotamian plain. Along these the stream of increasing commerce flowed, and from it Solomon could take his toll. He amassed wealth and developed power such as had never been known in Israel before. Recent excavations have shown the extent of the royal residence he built for himself at Megiddo, with its stables for chariot horses; and at the southern tip of his dominion at Elath on the Gulf of Aqabah he opened copper mines and built furnaces and shelters; and from Ezion-geber his trading ships went out to ports in southern Arabia and perhaps beyond. Moreover, he made treaties with Hiram, king of Tyre, so that exports from Israel could go out through Tyre and Sidon on Phoenician ships that controlled the trade across the Mediterranean Sea; and through Hiram he got wood for his buildings from the great cedars of Lebanon, and also craftsmen of special skills.

The impression made by Solomon through his ability and his increasing wealth is reflected in the First Book of Kings in the story of the visit of the Queen of Sheba. She herself was the ruler of one of the provinces in Arabia from which spices and other rich products came. She made a royal visit to Israel with a very great retinue, and she was left speechless with admiration at what she saw. Well she may have been if the actual magnificence of Solomon even began to justify the glamorous report of it that has come down in the Book of Kings. For according to that tradition, the palace that Solomon had built for himself had in it an ivory throne approached by six steps at the sides of which were sculptured lions; his bodyguard had shields of beaten gold; and the luxury and display around him came from as far as Africa and Spain, in cargoes that included gold, silver, ivory, apes and peacocks. No wonder therefore, that the Queen of Sheba should exclaim, "I did not believe the reports until I came and my own eyes had seen it. The report was true—and the half was not told me."

As Solomon's wealth became legendary, so did his reputation for wisdom. The Queen of Sheba had heard of that too, and one of her interests in coming was "to test him with hard questions."

It was a hard question that Solomon had to answer on the occasion that afterward became most famous. Two women were brought before him for judgment. They lived in the same house and each of them had a baby. But one baby died, and each woman declared that the living baby belonged to her. Who could know which told the truth, and which was lying?

Solomon listened to their claims and their denials.

One of the two said, "We were alone. There was no one else with us in the house. And this woman's son died in the night. And she arose at midnight and took my son from beside me while I slept and laid it in her bosom and laid the dead child in my bosom. When I rose in the morning to nurse my child, it was dead; but when I looked at it closely, it was not the child that I had borne."

The other woman said, "No, the living child is mine, and the dead child is yours."

And the first one cried, "No, the dead child is yours, and the living child is mine."

Solomon looked at them both. "Bring me a sword," he said.

The sword was brought. "Divide the living child in two," said Solomon, "and give half to the one, and half to the other."

"Oh, my lord," cried the woman who had spoken first, "give her the child. Do not slay it!"

But the other said, "It shall be neither mine nor yours; divide it."

"Give the living child to the first woman," said Solomon. "She is the mother." He had brought out the emotion that told the truth.

Besides Solomon's wealth and his wisdom, there was a third fact that made his reign most memorable for the people of Israel. He determined to build at Jerusalem a temple that should be the central shrine of the nation's worship. In the fourth year of his reign he started it, and for seven years the work went on. For its woodwork, cypress and cedar were brought from Lebanon, some of it to be carved and overlaid with gold. No building so splendid had been known in the land before, and the tradition of its glory lasted long after the then distant time of war and disaster in which the building itself would be destroyed. The Book of Kings which gives the story of Solomon was compiled, some three centuries later, by priests whose life and interest centered in the temple, and therefore Solomon seemed to them a great religious figure. They attributed to him the prayer of dedication of the temple, which is one of the noblest utterances in all the scriptures. And whether or not Solomon offered that prayer, it represents what the soul of the nation would have had him say:

> "O Lord, God of Israel, there is no God like thee, in heaven above or on earth beneath, keeping covenant and showing steadfast love to thy servants who walk before thee with all their heart. Will God indeed dwell on the earth? Behold, heaven and the highest heaven cannot contain thee; how much less this house which I have built. Yet have regard to the prayer of thy servant, that thine eye may be open night and day toward this place, the place of which thou hast said 'My name shall be there.' And hearken thou to the supplication of thy servant and of this people Israel, when they pray toward this place; yea, hear thou in heaven thy dwelling place; and when thou hearest, forgive."

CHAPTER THIRTY-FOUR

Rebellion,
and the Kingdom Divided

T HUS IT could have seemed that the reign of Solomon brought to Israel only benefit and blessing. But there were other facts which had a different character.

Solomon had built the temple to the God of Israel; but he married foreign wives, and some of them brought the practice of their own foreign worship with them. This harem of many women was not only an evidence of his fleshly passions; it was a betrayal of the religious loyalty he was supposed to have, for it was written of him that as he grew older "his wives turned away his heart after other gods."

Solomon also had brought magnificence to the land. People might be proud of what they saw—great buildings going up, wealth accumulating, a chance for even ordinary people to share in the prosperity that had come with Solomon's power. But meanwhile that power was turned into oppression. When Solomon wanted workers he sent out and conscripted them. There should be no more stubborn independence of tribes or of individuals either. He appointed twelve officials who were to collect tribute from their districts, and call into the king's service whatever able-bodied men they thought he wanted. So the king's buildings went up, rich food was brought to his banquet tables, the horses that filled his stables were groomed, the copper mines were dug, the ships that carried their cargoes down the Red Sea were loaded—but underneath all that a deep and sullen resentment began to grow. Out of that disaster would come to Solomon's kingdom.

There was a young man named Jeroboam who had been made responsible for recruiting the forced labor from one of the districts into which Solomon had divided the land. On a road out of Jerusalem he came face to face with Ahijah, who was called a prophet—in whom the smouldering anger of the people had begun to burn as a fire that was to him the wrath of God. Ahijah took the garment he was wearing and tore it into twelve pieces.

He said to Jeroboam, "Take these ten pieces. For this is the word of the Lord God of Israel, 'I am about to tear the kingdom from the hand of Solomon and will give you ten tribes. You shall be king over Israel.' "

When this came to Solomon's ears, he tried to seize Jeroboam and to kill him. But Jeroboam fled into Egypt. And before he had been there long, the news came that Solomon was dead.

Rehoboam, Solomon's son and heir, was anointed king at Shechem. But back from Egypt now came Jeroboam. He went to the new king and he said to him, "Your father made our yoke heavy. Now therefore lighten the hard service of your father and his heavy yoke upon us, and we will serve you."

Rehoboam would have done well to heed. But all he said was that if Jeroboam came back in three days he would give him an answer.

Then Rehoboam began to consult some of the men who had been close to Solomon. He turned first to those who were older and more experienced. "How do you advise me to answer these people?" he asked. They told him that he had better change his father's policies, and let the common people see that the new king had some concern for their well-being.

But Rehoboam had inherited his father's arrogance of power without his father's sense. He turned to some of the young bloods who were around him, and he asked them, "What do *you* advise that we answer these people who have said to me, 'Lighten the yoke that your father put upon us'?"

They told him, "This is the way to answer them: 'My little finger is thicker than my father's loins. If my father laid on you a heavy yoke, I will add to your yoke. My father chastised you with whips, but I will chastise you with scorpions.' "

And that is what Rehoboam was stupid enough to say when Jeroboam came back to get his answer.

The word spread like flame through Israel. Men had had enough already of this new king, even if he was of the blood of the beloved David. The cry went up. "We have no inheritance in the line of Jesse. To your tents, O Israel!" One of Rehoboam's taskmasters was stoned to death, and Rehoboam himself had to flee in his chariot to Jerusalem. All the northern tribes revolted, summoned Jeroboam to their assembly, and made him king. The realm that Solomon had established in prosperity and seeming permanence was dismembered. Only the tribes of Judah and Benjamin supported Rehoboam, and what was left to him now as his kingdom was limited to the little fragment of territory around Jerusalem. The land that had been ruled by David and Solomon was controlled by Jeroboam. His kingdom took the name that had belonged to the whole people, and was called the kingdom of Israel.

Rehoboam's kingdom took its name from the stronger of the only two tribes included in it, and so became the kingdom of Judah. Its weakness was quickly made evident. Shishak, the pharaoh of Egypt, sent his armies against Jerusalem. They entered the city and looted it, carrying off the golden ornaments of the temple and of Solomon's palace, and the shields of gold that belonged to Solomon's guard; so that in place of the former splendor Rehoboam's royalty was henceforth only a shabby thing.

Meanwhile Jeroboam was strengthening his control of the north. He realized at once that the temple which Solomon had built could be a sort of magnet to keep the people's thoughts drawn toward Jerusalem. He wanted to keep their life and loyalty within the limits that he controlled. So he set up new shrines at Bethel and at Dan, and he put up images there which were like the sacred bulls of Egypt and like the fertility gods which belonged to the old Canaanite idolatries that still lingered in the land. To the priests of the temple at Jerusalem who ultimately shaped the record as it was written in the Book of Kings, that seemed the ultimate apostasy; and all the disasters which came afterwards to the kingdom of Israel were ascribed to "the sins of Jeroboam which he sinned and which he made Israel to sin."

The death of Solomon and the rebellion against Rehoboam took place in 922 B.C. For the next two centuries, the relationship between the two separated kingdoms was a confused and changing one, often of hostility, sometimes of alliance against some external enemy that threatened them both. There were ugly periods when conditions in one or the other kingdom fell almost into anarchy, with rivalries for power, revolts against the reigning king, and even assassinations. Only occasionally did some ruler emerge who could command allegiance.

Yet the territory of the northern kingdom still included the narrow land bridge between the Mediterranean Sea on the west and the desert on the east over which the caravans between Egypt and Damascus and the rich cities of the Tigris and Euphrates valleys had to travel. When there was a king of Israel strong enough to maintain his borders he could take profitable toll on the roads along which the continual stream of laden camels carried the commerce of the busiest regions of the African and Asian worlds.

About a half century after the death of Solomon and the division of the kingdom, there arose in the north the first significant figure after Jeroboam. His name was Omri. He was the commander of the army of Israel. With the support of the troops he rose against Zimri, a conspirator who had killed the previous king and had himself held the throne for exactly seven days. Omri quickly proved himself to be a man astute in policy and resolute in action. He made an alliance with Phoenicia, and married his son to the daughter of the Phoenician king. He fought successfully against Syria to the north and Moab across the Jordan. Also on a strategic hill top he built his capital city of Samaria, and he developed there an opulence of life that began to parallel the luxury of Solomon. The dynasty he established became so significant that inscriptions in the empire of Assyria for a long time after his death and the death of his son and successor referred to the kingdom of Israel as the "land of the house of Omri."

CHAPTER THIRTY-FIVE

Elijah, the Prophet, Appears

O MRI WAS followed on the throne by Ahab; and Ahab's reign was made conspicuous not so much by anything he did himself as by two powerful figures who in different ways determined his destiny. One of them was his wife, Jezebel, a princess from Tyre, and the other was the first of the great prophets, Elijah.

Jezebel was to prove herself a figure as formidable as she was evil. She had a scornful contempt for the religion of Israel. What she wanted to see established was the worship of Baal, the god who was supposed to bring fertility to the land. She surrounded herself with priests of Baal, and as far as she could, she saw to it that those who stood for the worship of the God of Israel were killed.

Jezebel, with her stronger will, could dominate Ahab. But confronting them both was Elijah. Nothing is told of him before his abrupt appearance, and there is no description of him then except for his name and country—"Elijah the Tishbite, of Tishbe in Gilead." Suddenly he stands before Ahab, and from that moment he begins to tower above the circumstances of the time as a great mountain towers above the plains. And as the height of a mountain draws the clouds to gather round its summit, so the greatness of Elijah made legends gather round the central facts of what he did. Elijah represented the religion of the Covenant which had come down from Moses—the religion that included the Ten Commandments and the moral law; and now in him this religion of the Covenant would have its mortal combat with the corrupting worship of the Baal gods. Details of the Elijah story as it is told in the Book of Kings may represent therefore the marveling enlargement of tradition, but at the center of it is the solid fact of the man who had about him a power above the powers of this earth.

When he first appeared before the startled Ahab, Elijah declared, "As the Lord the God of Israel lives, there shall be neither dew nor rain these years, except by my word." Having said that he vanished as quickly as he had come—to the other side of the Jordan River. The drought he had predicted came, and there began to be famine in all the land. But it was told concerning Elijah that the voice of the Lord had promised, "I have commanded the ravens to feed you there"; and where Elijah went, others also should not lack.

He made his way to a town called Zarephath, and near its gate he found a woman, who was a widow, gathering sticks. He asked her to give him a little water to drink, and as she was going to get it, he called after her, "Bring me a morsel of bread in your hand."

But the woman answered, "As the Lord your God lives, I have nothing baked, only a handful of meal in a jar, and a little oil; and now I am gathering a couple of sticks that I may go in and prepare it for myself and my son—that we may eat it, and then die."

But Elijah told her to have no fear. She should go and bring him something to eat, and all would be well for her and for her son. God would see to it that they should not lack. So the woman went and did according to Elijah's word. Then Elijah stayed at the woman's house with her and her son for many days, yet "the jar of meal was not spent, neither did the cruse of oil fail, according to the word of the Lord which he spoke by Elijah."

After that the widow's son fell ill, and she was frantic in her grief and fear. She thought that somehow Elijah was responsible. "What have you against me, O man of God?" she cried. "You have come here to bring my sin to my remembrance, and to cause the death of my son!"

But Elijah said, "Give me your son."

He took the child from her arms and carried him to the upper room where he had been staying. He laid the child upon his bed and he prayed God to bring him back to life and strength. Then the child revived, and Elijah carried him down and gave him to his mother. "See, your son lives," he said; and the woman cried out, "Now I know that you are a man of God, and that the word of the Lord in your mouth is truth!"

All this while the drought and the famine were growing worse. Ahab had been hunting for the grim prophet who had predicted it, but he could not find him. He had sent one of his servants, Obadiah, to try to find streams or springs where there might still be water. And as Obadiah went on his way, there before him stood Elijah.

Obadiah fell on his face in astonishment and in awe. "Is it you, my lord Elijah?" he exclaimed. And the prophet answered, "It is I. Go tell your lord, 'Behold, Elijah is here.' "

Then Obadiah was terrified. Go and tell Ahab that Elijah was near and that he could be seized—Elijah whom Ahab had been scouting the whole land to find? Tell him that, and then have Elijah disappear? Was *this* what might happen? If it did happen, then the first thing Ahab would do would be to kill Obadiah in fury at Obadiah's false report.

But Elijah said, "As the Lord of hosts lives, I will certainly show myself to him today."

Obadiah went and carried the message, and after him came Elijah. Once again he confronted Ahab.

"Is it you, you troubler of Israel?" the king exclaimed.

But Elijah answered that it was not he who troubled Israel. Instead, it was Ahab and Ahab's family, because they had forsaken the commandments of the Lord and set up the worship of the Baal gods. Now, said Elijah, let Ahab send and summon all the Baal priests, and especially those that Jezebel had brought; and Ahab should see who was God in Israel.

Ahab therefore summoned the Baal priests to Mount Carmel, and a great crowd of people flocked around. "How long will you go limping between two opinions?" Elijah demanded of them. "If the Lord is God, follow him; but if Baal, then follow him." The crowd stood silent, without a word to say.

"I, even I only, am left as a prophet of the Lord," said Elijah, "and Baal's priests are four hundred and fifty men." Let the four hundred and fifty show, then, what they could do. Let a bull be given to him, Elijah said, and another bull to the Baal priests. The body of each bull should be put upon an altar, with no fire underneath. Then he would call upon God, and the Baal priests could call upon Baal; "and the God who answers by fire, he is God."

Now the people found their voice, and shouted in approval. Here was the kind of test that could stir excitement in any crowd.

Let the Baal priests begin, Elijah said. So they prepared their sacrifice, and they cried "O Baal, answer us!" From morning on until noon they kept up their incantation, but there was no voice or sign of answer.

Elijah taunted them. "Cry louder!" he said. Perhaps the Baal god was off on a journey, or perhaps he was asleep and needed to be awakened.

The Baal priests began to cut themselves with swords and lances and their chant increased in frenzy; but nothing happened as the hours went by and evening came.

Then said Elijah to the people, "Come near to me." He built up again an altar to the Lord that had been broken down, he put the sacrifice upon it and wood underneath, and he made the people pour water on the altar and on the wood. "Do it a second time," he said; and "Do it a third."

Elijah drew near the altar, and he prayed: "O Lord, God of Abraham, Isaac, and Israel, let it be known this day that thou art God in Israel, and that I am thy servant, and that I have done all these things at thy word. Answer me, O Lord, answer me, that this people may know that thou, O Lord, art God, and that thou hast turned their hearts back again!"

Above the staring crowd lightning flashed, and a bolt of fire struck the sacrifice and wrapped it in instant flames. And when the people saw it, they fell on their faces and cried, "The Lord, he is God; the Lord, he is God!"

"Seize the priests of Baal," said Elijah, "let not one of them escape." So the people seized them, and by the brook, Kishon, put them all to death.

Elijah turned to Ahab. "There is a sound of the rushing of rain!" he said. Up to the top of Mt. Carmel he went, and he said to his servant, "Go, look toward the sea."

But the servant answered, "There is nothing."

"Go again seven times," Elijah commanded.

At the seventh time the servant called, "Behold, a little cloud like a man's hand is rising out of the sea." And Elijah said, "Go, say to Ahab, prepare your chariot and go down, before the rain stops you."

In a little while the sky was black with clouds and wind, and the air was filled with drenching rain. Ahab drove toward the city of Jezreel along the flooded road, and Elijah, with his robe girded about his waist, ran before him. The drought which the prophet had predicted had been brought now to its end, according also to his word.

So the story of Elijah—passed on from generation to generation in the tradition which enlarged its drama—came to what seemed its triumphant climax. The one lonely prophet of God had preached against the Baal priests and had overawed a king.

CHAPTER THIRTY-SIX

The Champion
of the Common Man

B UT THE end of the story was not yet in sight. Still to be reckoned with was the implacable Jezebel. And when Jezebel heard of the death of the priests of Baal, she sent a messenger to Elijah to say to him, "So may the gods do to me, and more also, if I do not make your life as the life of one of them by this time tomorrow."

Then suddenly there came to Elijah the collapse which can follow a time of terrific stress and tension. Unknowingly, he had burned up his last reserves of strength. He alone had confronted the Baal priests and Ahab; but now there swept over him the desolating sense of that aloneness. How long could he keep up the solitary fight when all the odds seemed to be against him? Would there be any use in it at last? He fled for his life toward Beersheba, in Judah; and there in a barren place he sat down and prayed that he might die. He told the Lord that he had had enough. "Now take away my life, for I am no better than my fathers."

When some food that was given to him had restored his strength enough to travel farther, he went all the way to Horeb. And there in that same region of Sinai where the revelation had come to Moses, Elijah had his own new experience of the presence of God.

There among the grim mountains he was sheltered in a cave when there came one day an earthquake; and after the earthquake such a wind as seemed to split the very rocks, and after the wind the awful lightning. But neither the earthquake nor the wind nor the lightning made the lonely prophet feel any nearer to God.

Then it was as though he heard "a still small voice"; and he wrapped his face in his mantle and went and stood in the entrance of the cave. The Voice said, "What are you doing here, Elijah?"

Out of the depths of his spirit he answered: "I have been very jealous for the Lord, the God of hosts; for the people of Israel have forsaken thy covenant, thrown down thy altars, and slain thy prophets with the sword; and I, even I only, am left; and they seek my life to take it away."

But the Voice had something more important to deal with than the prophet's complaint. What had plunged Elijah into despair was the fact that he had left the place of duty, and that he had thought himself to be alone when he was not alone. There was work waiting for him to do for God. The Voice told him what it was, and told him to go back from this ignominious flight and begin to do it. It would not be in vain. He would find in Israel seven thousand others who would not bow the knee to Baal.

Meanwhile Ahab had been at war with Benhadad, king of Syria; and though he fought the war successfully, the result of it was confused, so that Ahab at the end of it was sullen and resentful. And now again appeared Elijah.

Next to the grounds of Ahab's palace there was a vineyard that belonged to a man named Naboth. Ahab tried to buy it, but Naboth would not sell. "The Lord forbid," he said, for the vineyard was an inheritance of his family. In frustrated disappointment and in petulance, Ahab went back to his house and lay on his bed and would not eat.

But Jezebel was of a different sort. Naboth would not sell his vineyard at the bidding of the king? Well, she would see to that. Let Ahab have no concern. "I will give you the vineyard of Naboth the Jezreelite," she said to him.

Then what she did was to write letters to some of the nobles of Ahab's court and sign them with the king's seal. In these letters she gave instruction that Naboth should be accused of blasphemy against God and treason to the king, and two disreputable liars were made to swear to the charges drawn up against him. So Naboth was condemned, taken out and stoned to death.

When the report of this was brought to Jezebel, she went in to Ahab. "You can get up now and go and take possession of Naboth's vineyard," she said. "He would not sell it to you for money. Now he is dead."

Ahab rose, and went out to the vineyard. But at the gate stood the one figure his conscience could not dare to face. There before him was Elijah.

"Have you found me, O my enemy?" Ahab said. And terrible in righteous indignation, Elijah answered, "Yes, I have found you!"

Then the prophet went on to denounce the evil which stood naked in the sight of the Lord, and to pronounce judgment and doom on Ahab and all his house. And when Ahab heard it he rent his clothes and put on the sackcloth of would-be repentance.

But whatever repentance he thought he sought did not go deep. The time was near at hand when he should meet the doom that Elijah had declared would come.

Queen Jezebel confronts Jehu, the conqueror and killer.

Jeremiah hears the word of God, "Whatsoever I command thee thou shalt speak."

CHAPTER THIRTY-SEVEN

The End of Ahab
and of Jezebel

N OT LONG after Elijah's word of judgment, Ahab launched a
war against the king of Syria to try to capture the city of
Ramoth-Gilead, and Jehoshaphat, king of Judah, was his ally.
Jehoshaphat wanted to find out what might be the omens for
success. So Ahab called together four hundred men supposed to
be religious seers and he asked them "Shall I go to battle against
Ramoth-Gilead, or shall I not?" And the whole company of these
so-called prophets said in chorus what they knew well enough
that Ahab desired to hear, "Go up to Ramoth-Gilead and triumph,
the Lord will give it into the hand of the king."

Jehoshaphat had sense enough to see the way the wind was
blowing. "Is there not some other prophet of the Lord," he asked,
"of whom we may inquire?"

Yes, there was one other, Ahab admitted, Micaiah, the son of
Zineah. "But I hate him," said Ahab, "for he never prophesies
good concerning me, but always evil."

All the same, Jehoshaphat thought that they ought to hear from
this Micaiah, and Ahab sent and had him brought. The messenger
who took the summons to him tried to give him prudent advice.
He told him that all the other prophets had promised Ahab success, and Micaiah had better do the same. But "As the Lord lives,
what the Lord says to me, that I will speak," Micaiah answered.

When he had come before Ahab, Ahab asked the question he
had asked before. Should he go up against Ramoth-Gilead? "Yes,
certainly," was Micaiah's answer. Let Ahab go up and prosper.

"How many times shall I adjure you to speak to me nothing but the truth in the name of the Lord?" said Ahab.

The truth? That was not what Ahab had generally welcomed. Let him see how he liked what would be the truth this time. "I saw all Israel scattered upon the mountains, as sheep that have no shepherd; and the Lord said, 'These have no master; let each return to his home in peace.' "

Ahab turned to Jehoshaphat: "Didn't I tell you," he said, "that he would not prophesy good concerning me, but only evil?"

Micaiah had not finished. Once more he would warn this king who wanted to listen only to good things. He said he had had a vision of the throne of God, and of a conversation that went on between the spirits gathered there. And the result of it was that Ahab should be tested by a false promise put into the mouth of the so-called prophets to whom he chose to listen.

One of them came up and struck Micaiah in the face. "This is the way the spirit of the Lord speaks from me to you!" he said. And Ahab turned furiously to his guards, "Put this fellow in prison," he commanded, "and feed him with scant fare of bread and water, until I come in peace."

Then Ahab and Jehoshaphat went out to the attack on Ramoth-Gilead. Notwithstanding his own bravado, Ahab had been made afraid by Micaiah's words; he took off his royal insignia and went into the battle disguised. The brunt of the battle fell at first therefore upon the king of Judah, while the Syrians who wanted above all to strike down Ahab could not distinguish which was he. But a chance arrow struck him beneath his breastplate. "Turn about," he said to the driver of his chariot, "and carry me out of the battle, for I am wounded." And when Ahab was propped in his chariot and his blood dripped upon its floor, the battle turned against the army of Israel and Judah, and at sunset the cry went up, "Every man to his own city and his country," and the rout began.

With the day's end, the wounded Ahab died, and they buried him in Samaria. The blood-stained chariot was washed at the pool of Samaria, and dogs licked up the blood. The awful words of judgment which Elijah had spoken at the gate of Naboth's vineyard were beginning to be fulfilled.

But though Ahab was dead, the reckoning with the evil that had gathered round him was not finished. He was succeeded on the throne by his son Joram. When Joram had reigned some twelve years, he was wounded—as his father had been—in battle against the Syrians, yet only lightly, so that he was recovering. But one of his troop commanders, named Jehu, became the center of an army revolt; and by influences set in motion by Elijah was anointed to be king. Joram did not know of it and he was in the city of Jezreel where he had gone for the healing of his wound.

A watchman on a tower of the wall of Jezreel reported that a chariot and its escorts were approaching, and Joram ordered a horsemen to ride out and see whether this was friend or foe. The horseman went and he asked his question, "Is it peace?"; and the man in the chariot answered, "What have you to do with peace? Turn around and ride behind me."

Joram sent out another horseman who asked the same question and got the same reply. And again the watchman on the wall of Jezreel reported to Joram, "He reached them, but he is not coming back."

Who was it in that chariot who was not allowing those messengers to return? The watchman looked and he gave the name which has become a by-word in language from that time to this: "The driving is like the driving of Jehu," he said, "for he drives furiously."

"Make ready," said Joram, so his servants harnessed his chariot. Joram drove out to meet Jehu, accompanied by his cousin Ahaziah, king of Judah, who was visiting him.

"Is it peace, Jehu?" Joram asked as the two men met.

"What peace can there be," Jehu retorted, "so long as the harlotries and the sorceries of your mother Jezebel are so many?"

"Treachery, Ahaziah!" said Joram beneath his breath to the king of Judah; and he turned and fled.

But Jehu drew his bow with his full strength and shot Joram between his shoulders, so that the arrow pierced his heart and he sank down in his chariot. "Pick up his body and throw it on the ground that belonged to Naboth the Jezreelite," said Jehu.

Ahaziah of Judah had fled with Joram. "Shoot him also," said Jehu. So Jehu's men pursued him and shot him in his chariot. His servants got him as far as Megiddo, but there he died.

The death of Ahaziah was only a casual matter for Jehu. The final target of his vengeance was still to be reached. Before he entered the city, the old queen-mother heard of what was happening. Scornful and imperious to the end, Jezebel painted her eyes and adorned her hair and stood at a window. "You murderer of your master!" she said to Jehu as he came in sight.

"Who is on my side?" Jehu called. Two or three servants looked out at him from back of the window. "Throw her down," he commanded. So they threw her down, where her blood spattered upon the wall, and where the horses trampled upon her. And when later, after he had sat down to eat and drink, Jehu said, "Go bury this cursed woman, for she is a king's daughter." His servants could find only her bones to bury, for the wild dogs had torn her body to pieces. The doom pronounced upon the house of Ahab had been completed.

CHAPTER THIRTY-EIGHT

The Healing of
Naaman the Syrian

ELIJAH'S LIFE drew to its end. He had cast his mantle upon a
young man, Elisha, who was to be his disciple and his successor. His impact upon his time had been so tremendous that
people could not believe that he would die. It was told that one
day when Elijah said to Elisha, "Ask what I shall do for you before
I am taken from you." Elisha said, "I pray you, let me inherit a
double portion of your spirit." And Elijah said, "You have asked
a hard thing; yet, if you see me as I am being taken from you, it
shall be so for you; but if you do not see me, it shall not be so."
And as they still went on and talked, behold, a chariot of fire and
horses of fire separated the two of them. And Elijah went up by
a whirlwind into heaven. And Elisha saw it and he cried, "My
father, my father! The chariots of Israel and its horsemen!" Then
he saw Elijah no more.

Elisha was not so great a man as his master. Yet a portion of
Elijah's spirit did rest upon him, and he was to be a voice that
would be influential in the overthrow and setting up of kings.
As had been true of Elijah, he came to be regarded with such awe
that the account of his life is filled with stories of miracles which
he was said to have performed.

Of these the most significant was one that was not most startling.
It was memorable instead because it showed a conception of God
different from what had existed in the days before Elijah. In
earlier generations it had often been supposed that the God of
Israel belonged to Israel only, and had no concern for other
peoples. But it had been to Zarephath in the alien territory of

Sidon that Elijah had first gone; and it was there that he brought food for the poor widow and healed her son. So also it was for a foreigner that Elisha would invoke the power of the Lord.

In the kingdom of Syria the commander of the Syrian army was a man named Naaman. He was a great person in the kingdom, a warrior of renown, and high in favor with the king. But he became a leper.

Now it chanced that in his household there was a little maid who had been brought back captive from Israel in one of the Syrian wars, and she waited on Naaman's wife. She said to her mistress, "If only my lord were with the prophet who is in Samaria! He would cure him of his leprosy."

When the king of Syria heard of that he said he would send a letter to the king of Israel. So he did send a letter, and with it rich presents. The letter was brief. What it said was this: "When this letter reaches you, know that I have sent to you Naaman, my servant, that you may cure him of his leprosy."

When the King of Israel read the letter he was dismayed. Who could cure a man of leprosy? "Am I God, to kill and to make alive?" he cried. The king of Syria had deliberately demanded the impossible in order to provoke a quarrel, he thought. When the demand could not be met, he might make it a pretext for war.

Elisha heard that the king of Israel had received the message that made him rend his clothes. "Send the man to me," he said, "that he may know that there is a prophet in Israel."

So Naaman came with his horses and chariots and halted at the door of Elisha's house. Elisha sent a messenger out to him. "Go wash in the Jordan seven times," he said, "and your flesh shall be restored, and you shall be clean."

Naaman was indignant, and he turned away. He said this prophet he had chosen to visit ought to have come out himself, and called on the name of his God, and shown what he could do. What was this message about going and bathing in the Jordan River? He could have washed in a river at home. "Are not Abana and Pharpar, rivers of Damascus, better than all the waters of Israel?" he said.

But some of his servants tried to persuade him. "If the prophet had commanded you to do some great thing, would you not have done it?" they asked him. How much simpler, then, when all that Elisha bade him do was to go and bathe in the Jordan.

Naaman yielded. He did go and dip himself seven times in the river, according to Elisha's word. And his flesh was restored like the flesh of a little child, and he was clean.

Back to Elisha then he came, with all his retinue. "Behold," he said, "I know now that there is no God in all the earth but in Israel," and he begged Elisha to accept a present from him.

But Elisha would take nothing.

Then Naaman made what might seem a strange request. Would Elisha let him take as much earth from near Elisha's house as two mules could carry? He said that when he went back to Damascus he would have to go with the king to bow in the temple of the god Rimmon—and for that might he be forgiven! But meanwhile on the earth that he would take back from Israel he would build himself a shrine in which he would worship the

God of Israel, since he then would be standing on ground that belonged to Israel's God. And so he went away with the two mules' burden of earth.

Thus for Naaman there was a happy ending. But not for someone else. When Gehazi, Elisha's servant, saw that his master had refused the gifts that Naaman had offered, he thought that he could seize a smart advantage for himself. He ran after Naaman, and Naaman turned when he saw him coming, and asked him "Is all well?"

Yes, everything was as it should be, Gehazi answered—and he had a message from Elisha. Since Naaman had left, two young men from a school of prophets had come to see Elisha. Would Naaman like to send a present for them—a talent of silver, and some clothes? Naaman said he would give two talents; and he did, not knowing that the money might get no further than Gehazi.

Gehazi went back to Elisha. Elisha looked at him. "Where have you been, Gehazi?" he asked. Gehazi said he hadn't been anywhere in particular. But Elisha answered, "Did I not go with you in spirit when Naaman turned from his chariot to meet you?" Gehazi could not hide what he had done. His punishment, said Elisha, should be that the leprosy which had been on Naaman the Syrian should cleave to him. And the story ends—"So Gehazi went out from his presence a leper, as white as snow."

CHAPTER THIRTY-NINE

The Prophet Who Could Not Be Silenced

J EHU, WHOM Elisha had helped to bring to the kingship, not only killed Ahab's son and Ahab's queen-Jezebel, but he went on with savage thoroughness to exterminate the entire line of those who were of the blood of Omri.

Furthermore he devised a cunning trap for those who represented the worship of Baal, which Jezebel had fostered in Israel. He assembled the people and said to them, "Ahab served Baal a little, but Jehu will serve him much," and he summoned all the priests of Baal to meet at the Baal temple. He said he intended to offer a great sacrifice to Baal, and anyone who failed to come to it would do so at his peril. When the Baal temple was filled from one end to the other with priests and worshippers, he surrounded it and blocked its doors with armed men. Then when the temple ritual was at its height, Jehu sent his order to the waiting swordsmen, "Go in and slay them; let not a man escape." They carried out that order, and they demolished the temple over the bodies of the dead. The sardonic "sacrifice to Baal" was complete.

Jehu's natural capacity for cruelty was plain enough. But his purge of all of Omri's dynasty and of the priests of Baal was linked also with a religious fanaticism which brought him support from men who thought they were serving God. In Israel there was a clan called the Rechabites. They had a fierce loyalty to the standards of life which belonged to Israel in the days when Moses and Joshua led the people in the desert. They dwelt in tents, and they despised the softness and the corruption which they associated with the settled land. So they were swung to Jehu's support when

Jehu—setting out of hunt down all of Jezebel's connections and to kill the priests of Baal—said to their leader, Jonadab, "Come with me and see my zeal for the Lord."

By blood and terror Jehu had established his authority in Israel, but in his reign he was to face increasing dangers. After what he had done to Jezebel, Phoenicia of course was hostile. The king of Syria attacked him from the north. And most ominous of all, the great empire of Assyria began to threaten him. On the Black Obelisk of Shalmaneser III, one of the sculptured tablets from the 9th Century B.C. which modern excavations have brought to light, Jehu is shown kneeling before the Assyrian king and bringing him his abject tribute.

But after the time of Jehu, the threat of Assyria was diverted by troubles at home, and new prosperity came to Israel. Trade along the caravan routes increased, and great wealth accumulated —though in the hands of the few, and not the many. Then in 786 B.C. there came to the throne the strongest man of the dynasty of Jehu, Jeroboam II. As a warrior he carried the borders of Israel in the north almost to Damascus, and in the south to the region of the Dead Sea. And in his capital city, Samaria, the rich lived in a luxury that seemed to bring back the days of Solomon.

But it was not Jeroboam himself who made his time most memorable. It was the appearance of one of the greatest of the prophets—the first of the prophets whose utterances were gathered into a book that bears his name. The Word of the Lord was to be more important than the passing events of history, and more enduring than the boasts of kings.

In the southern kingdom of Judah there was a man of God named Amos. He shepherded a few sheep in the desolate region below Jerusalem called the wilderness of Tekoa, and he was "a dresser of sycamore trees," which meant that he added to a scanty living by gathering the fig-like fruit which grew there. Nobody sponsored him, and no one needed to. In the empty lands and their wide silences, where few human footsteps came by day and only some wild beast on the prowl was heard by night, he watched "the seven stars and Orion" come up when the darkness fell, and brooded upon the majesty of God. He was apart from the noise and commotion of the nation's life, but he knew what was going on. Once in so often he would take his flocks to the markets, and especially to Bethel, just over the border in the northern kingdom, where the money-getting that marked the reign of Jeroboam II was most rampant. There the shepherd of Tekoa saw a civilization, greedy, grasping, self-indulgent, that seemed to him to have forgotten all the stern morality that had been learned at Sinai. There must be a voice to bring the cleansing Word of God, and Amos would be that voice.

He went to the central shrine at Bethel. To the crowd who had come to bring their sacrifices, he prophesied judgment on Israel and approaching doom. The righteousness of God had measured the structure of the nation's life, as a man with a plumb line measures a leaning wall; and the wall was about to crumble. Again he said that Israel was like a basket of summer fruit, still smooth and fair skin-deep, but rotting underneath. And all the pride of Israel, he said, was like a land about to be invaded by a swarm of locusts that would leave nothing growing there.

Amaziah, the priest, was outraged as Amos' denunciation grew more unmeasured each moment. He sent a message to Jeroboam, "Amos has conspired against you in the midst of the house of Israel, and the land is not able to bear his words. This is what he has said, 'Jeroboam shall die by the sword, and Israel must go into exile away from his land!' "

Toward Amos himself Amaziah turned with the contemptuous scorn which the high-placed priest supposed would be enough to dismiss this wild man who had appeared from nowhere. "You, seer, you!" he snarled. "Get back into the land of Judah where you came from. Earn your keep and prophesy there. But never open your mouth again at Bethel, for it is the king's sanctuary, and it is the temple of the kingdom."

Then Amos answered, "I was no prophet, nor a prophet's son; but I was a herdsman and a gatherer of sycamore fruit. The Lord took me from following the flock, and the Lord said to me, 'Go, prophesy to my people Israel.' Now therefore hear the word of the Lord!" And Amos launched not only upon Israel, but upon Amaziah himself, a prophecy of punishment more devastating than what had gone before.

What happened next we do not know. But one thing is certain. The message of Amos was not silenced, and his words have come down the centuries as part of Holy Scripture to be read as long as time may last.

CHAPTER FORTY

Amos' Message, and Hosea's

T HERE WERE three things which were Amos' concern, and upon which he turned the awful light of the judgment of God.

One was the corruption that had spread through the everyday conditions of life. Prosperity was all very well, but it was the evil in it that the prophet saw. On the hill of Samaria the rich had built their winter houses and their summer houses, while the poor huddled where they could. Sleek women—Amos called them "cows of Bashan"—lay on couches of ivory, and drank too much wine. Their luxury was built on oppression and cruelty, by those who had "turned justice to wormwood, and cast down righteousness to the earth." The powerful got advantages through bribes, while the common people had no justice. Wheat was sold mixed with chaff. There were crooked weights and measures in the marketplace, and the needy were sold into debt for the price of a piece of bread. For that brutal indifference to the sufferings of the poor there should come woe to those who were "at ease in Zion." "Shall not the land tremble on this account," Amos demanded, "and everyone mourn who dwells in it?"

The second thing that called down the prophet's condemnation was the hollow show of worship at the shrines. All the outward look of religion was there; large offerings, music, proper ritual; but it made no difference in the way the people behaved themselves the next day. To Amos that seemed a pretense which deserved nothing but the wrath of God; and in the name of God he said, "I hate, I despise your feasts, and I take no delight in your solemn assemblies. I will turn your feasts into mourning, and all your songs into lamentation."

The third thing that Amos saw was the assumption everywhere that no real calamity would ever fall on Israel, because Israel was "God's people" and their country was "God's country." Whenever God sifted the nations, Israel would come out on top, so the people thought, but Amos shocked them with his devastating contradiction. He would have them know that the God of Israel was also the Lord God of all mankind, and that all peoples should be weighed in his same righteous balances. To the crowd that listened to him in Bethel he described the judgments which would fall on the nations that Israel had hated—on Syria, on Tyre and Sidon, on Edom, Moab, Ammon and the Philistines. They wagged their heads in satisfaction when they heard that denunciation. But then Amos went on to his shattering climax.

"You only have I known among all the families of the earth," he said in the name of God. They had been given spiritual light and leading above all other peoples. So, his listeners thought, he would go on to say that they would be favored now above all others. No! "You only have I known," he repeated as from God, "therefore, therefore I will punish you for all your iniquities!"

So the prophecy of Amos was almost altogether a message of retribution and of doom. Israel had supposed it could look forward in bland confidence to the day of Judgment. But "Woe to you who desire the day of the Lord!" Amos said. "Why would you have the day of the Lord? It is darkness and not light." And to those in the crowd accustomed to softness he put the truth in terms of the harsh realities of the desert world he knew. Their attempt to evade the Judgment would be "As if a man fled from a lion, and a bear met him; or went into the house and leaned with his hand against the wall, and a serpent bit him."

The prophecies of Amos were spoken near the end of the long and glamorous reign of Jeroboam II. To all appearance, nothing seemed more unlikely than the disasters he had foretold becoming a reality. Jeroboam had been a great ruler, and his kingdom was richer than it had ever been. It seemed that all the skies were bright. But as a matter of fact, low down on the horizon to the east a black cloud was gathering. The terrible power of the armies of Assyria was about to move, and with its impact there would come the end.

Jeroboam died in 746 B.C. For the next quarter of a century there was chaos and violence, intrigue and assassination as one king claimed the throne and was pulled down by a successor. In this period there arose another prophet, not a man from the desert as Amos was, but one who lived in the midst of the civilization of the northern kingdom and therefore was identified with it to a degree of pity which the sterner Amos did not often feel.

The Book of his prophecy begins with an introduction that might seem incredible, "The word of the Lord that came to Hosea . . . When the Lord first spoke through Hosea, the Lord said to Hosea, 'Go, take to yourself a wife of harlotry and have children of harlotry, for the land commits great harlotry by forsaking the Lord.' "

Personal tragedy had come to Hosea himself; and this tragedy of his own was made for him a symbol of what he began to think of as the sorrow in the heart of God for the infidelity of his people. Hosea's wife had drifted away from him with miscellaneous lovers, until she became a prostitute at one of the Baal temples. How should Hosea treat her then? The human instinct would have been to let her remain an outcast. What right had such a woman to be reclaimed? But Hosea loved her still, and at length he brought her home.

As Hosea looked at the life of Israel, he saw in it the same evils that Amos had seen, and others also, because the order and control that had marked the reign of Jeroboam II had disintegrated now into near-anarchy. What Hosea saw was "swearing, lying, killing, stealing, and committing adultery; they break all bounds, and murder follows murder." Israel had boasted, said Hosea, "Ah, but I am rich, I have gained wealth for myself," but all the nation's riches could not offset the guilt it had incurred. What passed for worship did not penetrate the people's ordinary life; instead, that life, Hosea said, was "like a cake not turned"— like the flat hoe-cake that on one side seems to be cooked, but on the other side remains raw dough. And those who were supposed to be the leaders of religion were as guilty as the people generally. In the coming punishments, "It shall be like people, like priest," the prophet said; for "As robbers lie in wait for a man, so the priests are banded together; they murder on the way to Shechem, they commit villainy."

Hosea, like Amos, predicted the inevitable punishment which Israel must face. All the vain belief in the nation's prosperity and imagined power should be "like the morning mist, or like the dew that goes early away, like the chaff that swirls from the threshing floor or like smoke from a window." "They sow the wind," he said, "and they shall reap the whirlwind." The time would come when the people would "say to the mountains, cover us, and to the hills, fall upon us."

Yet Hosea, out of his own experience, believed in an ultimate compassion of God which the relentless prophecy of Amos had not expressed. If Israel would repent, there was still the everlasting mercy. Wistfully, Hosea reviewed the history of the breaking of the bonds in Egypt, the exodus, the long deliverance in the desert, as though he were thinking again the thoughts of God. "When Israel was a child, I loved him, and out of Egypt I called my son. It was I who taught him to walk. I took him up in my arms." God would open again a door of hope. And shifting to an analogy which came from the parallel of his unfaithful wife, Hosea heard God say to Israel, "I will heal their unfaithfulness," and "I will betroth you to me in faithfulness, and you shall know the Lord."

But Israel did not listen; or if it listened, its listening came too late. The terrible power of Assyria was on the march. Under Tiglath-Pileser III, it broke the resistance of Syria and stood at the borders of Palestine. Under his successor, Shalmaneser V, the kingdom of Israel was attacked, and Samaria, the capital besieged. For three years the city held out. Then in 721 B.C. it fell, and the whole kingdom was at the mercy of the Assyrians. Alien people were brought in to take possession of its land. Those of the defenders who were not slaughtered were carried away captive and mixed with the populations in the East. From that time on there would be mourning for "the lost ten tribes of Israel." Now that only the kingdom of Judah was left, those who had been called the people of Israel were henceforth to be called the Jews.

And Job said, "Let the day perish wherein I was born!"

Queen Esther risks her life as she goes in before the king.

Nebuchadnezzar's image of gold which all were commanded to worship.

"Then shall the Sun of righteousness arise with healing in his wings."

CHAPTER FORTY-ONE

Isaiah:
The Counsellor of Kings

T HE SOUTHERN kingdom of Judah would have a longer respite. The Assyrian armies marched south along the coastal plain to clash with Egypt, but they did not then attack Jerusalem. In Judah, for more than forty years from 783 B.C. there had been a King Uzziah, whose reign was almost as prosperous as that of Jeroboam II in the north. But in 742 he died a leper.

At the end of his reign there arose the prophet who in some respects would be considered the greatest in all the prophetic line, Isaiah, son of Amoz. In the sixth chapter of the Book that bears his name is the description of his call:

> In the year that King Uzziah died I saw the Lord sitting upon a throne, high and lifted up; and his train filled the temple. Above him stood the seraphim, each had six wings; with two he covered his face, and with two he covered his feet, and with two he flew. And one called to another and said:
>
> > "Holy, holy, holy is the Lord of hosts;
> > The whole earth is full of his glory."
>
> And the foundations of the thresholds shook at the voice of him who called, and the house was filled with smoke. And I said "Woe is me! for I am lost; for I am a man of unclean lips, and I dwell in the midst of a people of unclean lips, for my eyes have seen the King, the Lord of hosts."
>
> Then flew one of the seraphim to me, having in his hand a burning coal which he had taken with tongs from the altar. And he touched my mouth, and said: "Behold, this

has touched your lips; your guilt is taken away and your sin forgiven." And I heard the voice of the Lord saying "Whom shall I send, and who will go for us?" Then I said, "Here I am! Send me!"

Like Amos and Hosea, Isaiah saw how his nation had failed to respond to the purposes of God. In the name of the Lord he spoke a parable. When a man plants a vineyard and year by year finds no grapes there, nothing is left for him to do but to let the walls around it crumble and the vineyard itself be trodden down. So with the life of a people that seemed to bring forth little or nothing that was good. "O inhabitants of Jerusalem, and men of Judah," God was saying, "judge between me and my vineyard." God had "looked for justice, but behold, bloodshed; for righteousness, but behold a cry! Therefore, as the tongue of fire devours the stubble, and its dry grass sinks down in the flame, so their root will be as rottenness, and their blossom go up like dust."

And not only by a parable did Isaiah suggest the evils of the time. He set these forth in words that burned and blistered in their unsparing truth. There were those who were "heroes at drinking wine, and valiant men in mixing strong drink," but when it came to social justice they would "acquit the guilty for a bribe, and deprive the innocent of his right." They built their own luxurious houses, but the luxury in those houses was the spoil they had taken from the common people as they "ground the faces of the poor." So in the name of God the prophet voiced his warning and his command "Though you make many prayers, I will not listen. Your hands are full of blood. Wash yourselves, make yourselves clean; cease to do evil, learn to do good, seek justice, correct oppression, defend the fatherless, plead for the widow."

Isaiah not only preached to the people in general; for forty critical years he was counsellor to kings. It was a time of constant danger, for the Assyrian power which destroyed Samaria might at any day be let loose against Judah and Jerusalem. Uzziah was succeeded by Jotham, and Jotham by Ahaz. Both of these were like fluttering birds that saw the hawk and turned here and there in helpless search for safety. At the beginning of the reign of Ahaz, when Samaria had not yet fallen, the king of Syria and the king of Israel made an alliance against Assyria, and they marched against Jerusalem to compel Ahaz to join them—or else be supplanted by a puppet king whom they would set up. To Ahaz there seemed only two alternatives: either to yield and join the alliance, or else to send out a desperate appeal to Assyria itself to come to his defense.

While he hesitated, Isaiah came to him. The prophet poured scorn upon the conspiracy of Syria and Israel, "these two smoldering stumps of firebrands," and he counselled against any message to Assyria. Be quiet, he said to Ahaz, and have no fear. Stop twisting here and there toward panicky expedients, but trust in the God of Righteousness who will show himself to be the Lord of history. Before his eyes the kings of Syria and Israel were insignificant and Assyria would be an instrument of his hand. Isaiah promised Ahaz a sign—the sign that is described in the seventh and ninth chapters of the Book of his recorded prophecy. A child should be born in Judah who would share the distress that was to come upon the people, but through whom in the end there would be deliverance; a child whose name should be Immanuel, "God with us," and by whom the kingdom of David would be established "with justice and with righteousness, from this time forth and for evermore."

Isaiah stood above the tumult and confusion of the human threats that seemed so great, but which to him were only an eddy in the stream of time. Ahaz had only to wait for the unfolding of the saving purposes of God. But Ahaz would not listen. He went off to Damascus to make his ignominious plea to Tiglath-Pileser, the king of Assyria, to pay him tribute, and to bring back an altar of Assyrian worship and set it up in Jerusalem.

Ahaz died and was succeeded by Hezekiah. He got rid of the Assyrian altar in Jerusalem and he tried to cleanse the whole worship of the people from the corruptions which had crept into it. But as to Assyria his faith was not great enough to wait for God in his own way and time to break the pride of the aggressor. Egypt was stirring up war against Assyria, and Hezekiah proposed to align himself with Egypt. That would be short-sighted folly, said Isaiah, "a covenant with death." The supposed strength of Egypt would prove a broken reed, and the alliance only emptiness. Only if Judah by the manner of its living *deserved* to be delivered would deliverance come. "In returning and rest you shall be saved," the prophet said; "in quietness and in confidence shall be your strength."

Nevertheless, Hezekiah provoked Assyria; and immediately Sennacherib, the new king, launched his army against Jerusalem. As he boasted afterwards in one of his inscriptions, he shut up Hezekiah "like a caged bird." The commander of his besieging forces stood outside Jerusalem and taunted the people who, silent and terrified, looked down at him from the wall. He recited the names of the cities which Sennacherib's army had overrun, and he demanded the surrender of Jerusalem. "Hear the words of the great king, the king of Assyria," he shouted. "Do not let Hezekiah deceive you, for he will not be able to deliver you; nor mislead you by saying, 'The Lord will deliver us.' Where are the gods of Hamath and Arpad? Where are the gods of Sepharvaim? Have they delivered Samaria out of my hand? Who among all the gods of these countries have delivered their countries, that the Lord should deliver Jerusalem out of my hand?"

But now Isaiah made a surprising promise. To him Jerusalem represented more than just a Judean city. It was the shrine and symbol of God's special presence among the peoples of the earth. He had said that God would use Assyria to scourge Judah toward repentance for its sins. But it was God and not Assyria to whom the final power belonged. Now the boast of Assyria had gone too far. "Shall the axe vaunt itself over him who hews with it?" The Assyrian army should not prevail, and Jerusalem would not fall.

Exactly what happened is not clear. It may have been that a plague broke out in Sennacherib's camp. It may have been that report came to him of revolts in the heart of his empire. In any case, the basic fact was the sudden lifting of the siege. Sennacherib withdrew to Nineveh. There later, in the temple of his god, he was assassinated by two of his own sons.

After that deliverance of Jerusalem in 701 B.C., no more is told of what Isaiah did. But probably to the latter part of his ministry belong the prophecies which were his greatest message. Seeing that in the end disaster might fall upon Judah as a nation, as it had already fallen on Israel, he foretold a saving "remnant." And that remnant would "lean upon the Lord, the Holy One of Israel in truth." Even if the nation should be broken in pieces, the faithful would survive to be a spiritual church.

CHAPTER FORTY-TWO

Evil Times
and Attempted Reformation

A<small>T THE</small> death of Sennacherib his successor was Esarhaddon, and after him came Ashurbanapal, from 669 to 633 B.C. During the reign of Esarhaddon and in the first part of the reign of Ashurbanapal, the power of Assyria again increased until it became the mightiest empire that the world had known. All of western Asia as far as the Mediterranean was in subjection. Egypt was beaten and the Pharaoh taken captive, and later the tide of Assyrian conquest rolled deeper into the valley of the Nile and destroyed the ancient city of Thebes.

Meanwhile in Judah when Hezekiah died in 687 B.C., he was succeeded by his son Manasseh, whose long reign of more than forty years proved to be a period of almost unmitigated evil. Not only was the kingdom shamed by having to pay abject tribute to Assyria; it was corrupted religiously by Manasseh's repudiation of every reform that Hezekiah, his father, had tried to carry through. He permitted the unashamed return of Baal worship, with its female symbols also of the mother-goddess and its temple prostitutes; he let the old cult of the dead come back, with its mumbo-jumbo of mediums and magic; and as the lowest point of cruel paganism, he instituted human sacrifice. In the words of the Second Book of Kings, "he seduced the people to do more evil than did the nations whom the Lord destroyed."

· Yet not even Manasseh could stamp out all the better influences in Judah. At the temple in Jerusalem were priests, and here and there were men and women whose loyalty to the great religious heritage was too devoted for any reaction to destroy. The messages of the prophets in the previous century were remembered and repeated. In the time of Isaiah there had been his contemporary prophet, Micah, who lived in a little town, and unlike Isaiah, had no love for the great city. On the contrary, he regarded Jerusalem as the center in which the social evils of the people's life had become most flagrant, and upon which the judgment of God would surely fall. In the time of Manasseh, therefore, when even the temple in Jerusalem had been defiled by pagan altars, men recalled the grim prophecy of Micah:

> "Zion shall be plowed as a field
> Jerusalem shall become a heap of ruins."

Moreover, in what has been handed down as the Book of Micah, there is included the passage which has been remembered and repeated more than almost any other prophetic utterance. Although it is written on the same scroll with Micah's own un-questioned prophecies, it probably came not from Micah or his time but from out of the deep darkness of Manasseh's evil reign; and if so, it reveals that there was some anonymous but heroic figure who saw the saving truth that not even Manasseh's wicked-ness could blot out, and dared express it. "With what shall I come before the Lord, and bow myself before God on high?" he asked. "Will the Lord be pleased with thousands of rams, with ten thou-sands of rivers of oil? Shall I give my first born for my transgres-sion, the fruit of my body for the sin of my soul?"

And as against that parade of supposed religion, and against the savage superstition of child sacrifice of which Manasseh had been guilty, he gave his immortal answer, "He has showed you, O man, what is good, and what does the Lord require of you but to do justice, and to love kindness, and to walk humbly with your God."

At length Manasseh died, and Amon his son succeeded him. But after two years he was assassinated; and his heir, the boy Josiah, was only eight years old. It seemed that all the signs were ominous for the kingdom of Judah. About the time when Josiah had come of age, the prophet Zephaniah looked out upon his world and particularly upon the threat of invasion by Scythians from the north, and he foretold disaster.

"The great day of the Lord is near," he cried—"near and hasten-ing fast. A day of wrath is that day, a day of distress and anguish, a day of ruin and devastation, a day of darkness and gloom."

Yet as a matter of fact there was first to come a better period, like a shaft of sunlight breaking through clouds before they thickened again into a fatal storm. Josiah was of a completely different spirit from Manasseh, and he was quick to respond to an amazing discovery which happened about the middle of his reign. One day in the temple the priest, Hilkiah, came upon a scroll which no one knew was there. He sent it to King Josiah, and when Josiah began to read it, he rent his clothes in astonishment and distress. For what that scroll contained was a description of worship and faith as they were meant to be, so far removed from the facts of Josiah's time that the difference was shocking. When Hilkiah found it, he called it "the book of the law." It is embodied now among the Holy Scriptures as the Book of Deuteronomy. Exactly when it was written, and how long it had lain forgotten in the temple, no one could tell; but the substance of the Book reflected the convictions which controlled the life of Israel in the years when the descendants of Abraham first regarded themselves as the people with whom God had made his covenant.

"Hear, O Israel, the statutes and judgments which I speak in your ears this day, that you may learn them, and keep, and do them." That was what Josiah read. Then he read also, as having come down from Moses, the story of God's leading of the people out of Egypt, through the wilderness and into the Promised Land. Therefore they were to "love the Lord your God with all your heart, and with all your soul." To love God meant devotion to his purpose—his purpose of a life of moral uprightness according to the standards of the Ten Commandments. But Israel had been infected by the corruption of the pagan peoples, and even the temple at Jerusalem was defiled by altars to the pagan gods.

Shocked into a new awareness of the nation's religious failure, Josiah began what he meant to be a thorough reformation. He ordered the destruction of all the places where the Baal god and goddess had been worshipped. He put an end to prostitution at the shrines and to the abomination of human sacrifice. And he tried to centralize worship at the temple in Jerusalem and so prevent the abuses which had grown up at the local shrines.

CHAPTER FORTY-THREE

Assyria Falls Before the Power of Babylon

J OSIAH EVEN reached beyond his own borders and wiped out the rival temple at Bethel in the north. Earlier in the century no king of Judah would have dared to do that, for all of Palestine was subject to Assyria, and the ruler of Judah was only a puppet to move or keep still at Assyrian command. But the Assyrian empire had begun to break up because of its own immensity. It was too far flung to be held together. At about the time Josiah was born, revolts had begun to break out in Assyrian provinces. New enemies also were gathering around the borders of the empire— Scythians from beyond the Caucasus mountains, Medes in the highlands of Iran, a new and more determined Pharaoh in Egypt. Particularly in the Tigris and Euphrates valleys where the heart of the empire lay there was the rising power of Babylon. Near the end of the century Babylon in the south made alliance with the new king of the Medes to the northeast and laid siege to Nineveh, the Assyrian capital. In 612 Nineveh fell. The incredible had happened. The tyranny which had held half the civilized world in subjection was destroyed. The exultancy with which nations, long humiliated by Assyria, heard that news echoes in the terrific lines of the Old Testament Book of Nahum:

> Woe to the bloody city
>   all full of lies and booty—
> The crack of whip, and the rumble of wheel
>   galloping horse and bounding chariot!
> Horsemen charging
>   flashing sword and glittering spear

> hosts of slain,
>   heaps of corpses,
>   dead bodies without end!

> Where is the lion's den
>   the cave of the young lions
> Where the lion brought his prey
>   where his cubs were, with none to disturb?

> Behold, I am against you, says the Lord of hosts, and I will burn your chariots in smoke, and the sword shall devour your young lions; I will cut off your prey from the earth, and the voice of your messengers shall no more be heard.

But the destruction of Nineveh and the end of Assyrian power was not to bring in a better day for the kingdom of Judah. Josiah thought it would. He had dreams now of restoring what was remembered as the glory of the kingdom of David. When an Egyptian army marched north to advance Egyptian claims in the general break-up of the time, Josiah marched against it. They clashed in battle at Megiddo in 609 b.c. and in that battle Josiah himself was slain.

Egypt now put a puppet king to rule in Jerusalem. He was a son of Josiah named Jehoikim. He thought that with the backing of Egypt he was secure. But the dominance of Egypt was to be only a passing thing. On the horizon was the new power of Babylonia, which was to prove as brutal and menacing as the power of Assyria had been. Those in Judah who had hoped for some conspicuous deliverance were almost in despair, and their cry is heard in the words of the prophet Habakkuk:

> O Lord, how long shall I cry for help,
>   and thou wilt not hear?
> Or cry to thee "Violence!"
>   and thou wilt not save?
> Thou who art of purer eyes than to behold evil
>   and canst not look on wrong,
> Why dost thou look on faithless men
>   and art silent when the wicked swallows up
>   the man more righteous than he?

And at last: Habakkuk could cling only to a hope that was beyond the things he saw:

For still the vision awaits its time;
  it hastens to the end—it will not lie.
If it seem slow, wait for it,
  it will surely come, it will not delay.
Behold, he whose soul is not upright in him shall fail
  but the righteous shall live by his faith.

Another and greater prophet also had appeared in Judah. This was Jeremiah, "the son of Hilkiah, of the priests who were in Anathoth." He had begun to prophesy in the reign of Josiah, probably as early as 626 B.C. As Moses after his vision of the burning bush had shrunk from the dread commission of going back to Egypt and confronting Pharaoh, so Jeremiah shrank from the compulsion which came upon him almost from his boyhood to speak the word of God against a sinful people. "Ah, Lord God!" he cried, "Behold, I do not know how to speak, for I am only a youth." But the Lord said, "Do not say 'I am only a youth'; for to all to whom I send you you shall go, and whatever I command you you shall speak. Be not afraid of them, for I am with you to deliver you."

Before Josiah's attempted reformation, Jeremiah had seen the glaring need of it. He stripped away self-satisfied pretenses and showed the ugly facts of immorality and apostasy with a truthfulness as terrible as that of Amos and Isaiah. There were men, he said, like "well-fed lusty stallions, each neighing for his neighbor's wife." In their greed for their own profit they were "fat and sleek," indifferent to justice or the rights of the poor. "As a cage is full of birds, so are their houses full of deceit"; and that was how they had grown great and rich. Worst of all, what passed for religion had become hypocrisy. "The prophets prophesy falsely, and my people love to have it so."

Whatever results there were in Josiah's reformation faded when he was dead and Jehoiakim was king. In his character Jehoiakim was another Manasseh—time-serving, cruel, contemptuous of his people's religious heritage. In the first year of his reign there came to Jeremiah the divine command, "Stand in the court of the Lord's house, and speak to all the cities of Judah which come to worship in the house of the Lord all the words that I command you to speak to them; do not hold back a word."

CHAPTER FORTY-FOUR

Jeremiah's
Heroic Truthfulness

J EREMIAH WENT to the temple and launched the words that
would shake the kingdom like the tremors of an earthquake.
What were they trusting in? he asked the crowd that gathered
round him. Did they think that because they had what seemed the
signs of religion, these would be enough? "This is the temple of
the Lord, the temple of the Lord, the temple of the Lord"—that is
what they would be saying. But to their glib assurance, this was
what God's awful righteousness had to say:

> "Behold, you trust in deceptive words to no avail. Will
> you steal, murder, commit adultery, swear falsely, burn in-
> cense to Baal and go after other gods that you have not
> known, and then come and stand before me in this house,
> which is called by my name, and say 'We are delivered!'—
> only to go on doing all these abominations? Has this house,
> which is called by my name, become a den of robbers in
> your eyes?"

Then came the prophesy of judgment. Destruction should fall
upon Jerusalem, and the temple itself would not be spared. " 'Because you have done all these things,' says the Lord, 'therefore I
will do to the house which is called by my name and in which you
trust, as I did to Shiloh. And I will cast you out of my sight, as I
cast out all your kinsmen, all the offspring of Ephraim.' "

What had happened to the northern kingdom, and to its most
ancient sanctuary would happen now to Judah and to the temple.

178

"The dead bodies of this people will be food for the birds of the air, and for the beasts of the earth; for the land shall become a waste!"

Astonishment and anger ran through the crowd. Led by some of the priests, a gang laid hold of Jeremiah, shouting that they would kill him. How had he dared to prophesy that the temple should be "like Shiloh," and that Jerusalem should be left without inhabitants?

Jeremiah was not intimidated. "I am in your hands," he said. They might do with him what they chose. "But know for certain," he said, "that if you put me to death, you will bring innocent blood upon yourselves and upon this city and the inhabitants, for in truth the Lord sent me to you to speak all these words."

Then some men of moral authority made themselves heard. There had been a great prophet, Micah, long before who had predicted the fall of Jerusalem. Nobody had killed him. There was no sense, then, in killing this man.

So Jeremiah went free. He continued to preach, because, as he said, the word of God "was in my heart as a burning fire, and I am weary with holding it in, and I cannot." Only a little knot of friends stood by him, and for the most part he was in heartbreaking loneliness. Once he was put in the stocks, exposed to the contempt and ridicule of all the passers-by.

Meanwhile Jehoiakim thought he was safe on his throne because of protection by the Egyptian Pharaoh. But in 605 B.C. the armies of Egypt were crushed by the Babylonians in the battle of Carchemish. Now Jeremiah was moved again to speak. He dictated his prophecies to his friend and follower Baruch; and he had Baruch take the scroll on which the prophecies were written and go and read it aloud in the court of the Temple.

When some of the nobles of the court heard of what Baruch had done they sent for him and made him read again the scroll of Jeremiah's words. Looking at one another in fear, they said that the scroll must be read to the king. Jehoiakim was in his winter palace, sitting before a brazier on which a fire burned. A man named Jehudi read from the roll; and as he read, Jehoiakim snatched the parchment from him, cut off the part he had read, and threw it in the fire.

It was no wonder that the king was furious, because Jeremiah had predicted the conquest and destruction of the kingdom of Judah by the Babylonians and the death of Jehoiakim himself. He ordered the arrest of Jeremiah and of Baruch; but they had been warned, had hidden themselves and escaped.

For a time it seemed that Jehoiakim could shrug off the prophecy of Jeremiah as nothing but a lying threat. After the battle of Carchemish, no immediate danger developed. The Babylonian king, Nabopolassar, had died shortly after his victory; and his successor, Nebuchadnezzar, had to stop long enough to establish his own rule. When he was ready, he moved against Jerusalem. Before he had reached the city, Jehoiakim died. He was still the king and he therefore was given a royal funeral; but in the dreadful destruction and defilement that would shortly fall upon the city Jeremiah's prediction would come true, that "with the burial of an ass he shall be buried, dragged and cast forth beyond the gates of Jerusalem."

His eighteen-year-old son, Jehoiachin, succeeded him, in time only to see the city assaulted and captured by Nebuchadnezzar, and to be carried off a prisoner to Babylon.

Nebuchadnezzar looted the royal treasury and the temple, but he did not destroy the city. He left in it the part of the population that seemed to him too contemptible to bother with. All persons of importance he herded into exile along with Jehoiachin. He took Jehoiachin's uncle, Zedekiah, and left him in Jerusalem as a puppet king. And he left Jeremiah.

It might have seemed now that Jeremiah would not need to prophesy any more calamity. But he had already said that it was only false prophets who counselled "Peace, peace" when there was no peace. The outward danger might appear to have been abated; but the awful reckoning with the stubborn and stupid follies of Judah was not finished.

A new and ambitious Pharaoh was on the throne of Egypt, and he tried to enlist Phoenicia, Edom, Moab, Ammon and Judah in a new alliance against Babylon. Zedekiah was urged to enter it by shortsighted men who surrounded him. But Jeremiah read the facts of the time with a vision more profound. He knew that the proposed rebellion would only provoke the Babylonians to come back with devastating punishment. And he said they would come, and that Judah must surrender to its fate. He said this not just in calculation of political realities. He said it because of his vision of the ultimate purposes of God. This people of the covenant had been unfaithful. Prosperity had only made them forgetful and corrupt. Now for their soul's sake God must send them through a furnace of affliction. His terrible mercy must destroy the nation, that he might winnow out a remnant of the people who would be fit to be his witnesses in the world. So Jeremiah had to do what his own instinctive patriotism shrank from. He had to say that God would use the Babylonians to punish those who had liked to call themselves the people of God.

Zedekiah was not an evil man, as Jehoiakim had been; but he was confused and weak. When Jeremiah began to denounce alliance with Egypt and to predict the victory of Babylon, men at Zedekiah's court cried, "Treason!" Jeremiah was no better than an enemy within the gates. Fury broke out against him. He was arrested and put in prison.

Meanwhile, a Babylonian army was advancing and soon might be outside the walls. Jeremiah committed now what seemed to the men about the king to be his final outrage. He was declaring, "He who stays in this city shall die by the sword, by famine, and by pestilence; but he who goes out and surrenders to the Babylonians shall have his life as a prize of war." "He is weakening the hands of the soldiers and of all the people," his enemies cried. "Let this man be put to death!"

They demanded that of Zedekiah, and the harassed king said, "He is in your hands. I can do nothing against you." So they took Jeremiah and dropped him down a well where Jeremiah sank in foul mire at the bottom, and he would have died there, except that one man revolted from that spectacle and got some other men and pulled Jeremiah out.

Then the king sent secretly for Jeremiah. Plaintively he tried to get some encouragement from the prophet, but he could give him none of the sort he wanted. The city must surrender to the Babylonians, even though they would take terrible vengeance on it when it fell.

That was what Jeremiah had to say. Yet he did not say it willingly. If on his lips there was judgment, in his heart there was anguish. Like Hosea, he could understand not only the wrath but the long suffering of God. Beyond the oncoming darkness he could see the hope of a people purified at last. He showed his own trust in the long future in one extraordinary act. Knowing that any immediate deliverance from Babylon was impossible, he had nevertheless bought a vineyard in his native town of Anathoth and had had the purchase certified and sealed, as a sign that "houses and fields and vineyards shall again be bought in this land." And he who had so often been the prophet of doom had said also, "Keep your voice from weeping and your eyes from tears. There is hope for your future, says the Lord; and your children shall come back to their own country."

The inexorable events moved on to the climax which Jeremiah had foretold. Nebuchadnezzar captured Jerusalem, and this time he fully destroyed it. He put out Zedekiah's eyes and carried him away to Babylon.

Jeremiah remained in the ruins of Jerusalem, but the wretchedness there turned into anarchy. Some of those who were left determined to go down into Egypt, and they compelled Jeremiah to go with them. He had seen the destruction of the temple and of all the other outward religious forms in which his people trusted, but in his prophesy he had left this immortal promise:

"Behold, the days are coming, says the Lord, when I will make a new covenant with the house of Israel and the house of Judah, not like the covenant which I made with their fathers. But this is the covenant which I will make with the house of Israel: I will put my law within them, and I will write it upon their hearts; and I will be their God, and they shall be my people."

CHAPTER FORTY-FIVE

The Years of
Captivity and Exile

F OR THE Jewish exiles, shocked by the fall of Jerusalem and by
being carried as captives to Babylon, there were confused
emotions.

In the first place, there was almost despair. One of the great psalms expressed it:

> By the waters of Babylon,
>   there we sat down and wept,
> when we remembered Zion.
> For there our captors
>   required of us songs
> and our tormentors, mirth, saying
> "Sing us one of the songs of Zion!"
> How shall we sing the Lord's song
>   in a foreign land?
> If I forget you, O Jerusalem,
>   let my right hand wither!"

Or they mourned in the words of the Book of Lamentation:

> How lonely sits the city
>   that was full of people!
> How like a widow has she become,
>   She that was great among the nations!
> She that was a princess among the cities
>   has become a vassal.
> Judah has gone into exile because of affliction
>   and hard servitude;
> She dwells now among the nations
>   but finds no resting place.
> Is it nothing to you, all you who pass by?
>   Look and see
> if there is any sorrow like my sorrow
>   which was brought upon me
> which the Lord inflicted
>   on the day of his fierce anger.

But rising out of hopelessness there was also sometimes another mood. The old pride of nationalism was not broken, and the sullen anger of a defeated people smouldered. Not many could accept the fact that it was default of character and not conditions only that had led to the downfall of the Judean kingdom. If conditions could change, they thought, the former days would come again. Jehoiachin was still living. Something might happen to break the power of Babylon, and to bring Jehoiachin and the other exiles back to Jerusalem.

But as Jeremiah had spoken the chastening word of God in Jerusalem, so there was another prophet now in Babylon. This was Ezekiel. He had been brought there with the first group of exiles after the first attack upon Judah by Nebuchadnezzar in 597 B.C. His words were directed first to the Jews who were in Babylon, but his message went back also to those who still remained in what had been the kingdom of Judah. Sometimes by plain speech, sometimes by the ecstatic utterance of a man entranced by unearthly visions, and often by dramatic signs, Ezekiel denounced the expectation that Babylon might soon fall. To fasten thought on that, he said, was foolishness—and worse than foolishness. It was refusal to face the truth of God, whose purpose was that the soul of the people might be purified by suffering. Though they had been scattered among the countries, God could still be a sanctuary for them in the country where they had gone. And what they needed to pray for was not an easing of their lot, but the fulfillment of the promise God made to his people if they would listen and obey—"I will give them a new heart, and put a new spirit within them; I will take the stony heart out of their flesh and give them a heart of flesh, that they may walk in my statutes and keep my ordinances and obey them; and they shall be my people, and I will be their God."

So, together with his warnings, Ezekiel held out hope for the future when God's chastening would have done its work. There had come to him a vision. He stood in a valley full of dead bones, and the voice of the Lord said to him, "Son of man, can these bones live?" All Ezekiel could answer was, "O Lord God, thou knowest." Then the divine voice commanded him, "Prophesy to these bones, and say to them, O dry bones, hear the word of the Lord. Thus says the Lord God to these bones: Behold, I will cause breath to enter you, and you shall live."

So Ezekiel spoke as he had been commanded. Then in the valley there was a noise and a rattling; bone came together with

bone, and they were clothed with flesh. But as yet there was no breath in them. Then once more Ezekiel was bidden to speak— "Thus says the Lord God: Come from the four winds, O breath, and breathe upon these slain, that they may live." And breath came into them "and they lived, and stood upon their feet, an exceeding great host."

Not only in the vision but in fact, new breath did come to dead bones. It came in the very valley of that which had seemed only disaster and defeat. What had made the Jewish exiles mourn most was the destruction of the temple, and the thought that because of it they had lost their hold on God. But the worship in the temple had centered round animal sacrifice, and so brought always the danger that it might make the people trust in outward form. Now they were to learn—as Hosea had prophesied long before—that "the knowledge of God is more than all burnt offerings." Since there was no temple to go to, the exiles met together where they could; and so there developed the synagogue—which meant not a building, but the assembly of those who would worship God. They listened now to the reading of the law and the prophets. They confessed their sins and prayed. They remembered the Ten Commandments, and began to learn their central meaning—to love God, and to try to love one's neighbor.

So the synagogue was one of the greatest blessings that ever came to Jewry, and through the Jews a blessing to all the world. In all the centuries since that time, the synagogue has set the standards for Jewish life, and it became the example also for Christian worship. It gave new meaning to religion, because it tied the worship of God forever to morality and to righteousness of life.

CHAPTER FORTY-SIX

Light Breaks Through
the Darkness

HALF A century went by. All, or nearly all, of the generation
that had been brought as captives to Babylon were dead.
Many of their descendants had become accustomed to what had
been the alien land. After Nebuchadnezzar's death the rulers of
Babylon had treated these Jewish people tolerantly; so that most
of them found work and lived in their own houses. Increasing
numbers of them therefore were content to remain in Babylon.
But there were others whose hearts were hungry with desire for
the Holy Land which, to their deep loyalty, would forever seem
their home.

Then late in the 6th century B.C. there came events that shook
the world. In Central Asia there arose a great warrior and ruler,
Cyrus, king of Persia. His power rapidly increased. In 539 B.C.
he attacked Babylon, got through the river gates of the once-
mighty city, and put an end once for all to the Babylonian empire. Now it was Cyrus, and not Belshazzar the last king of
Babylon, who would determine the fate of the Jewish exiles.

Among the exiles arose the prophet who ranks as perhaps the
greatest in all the prophetic line. His prophesies were written
afterwards on rolls that held the prophesies of Isaiah, who had
lived in Hezekiah's time; and so for a long while it was forgotten
that there had been another prophet. Even now, no one knows
his name; but became his prophecies have come down as part of
the single Book of Isaiah, he is called the "second Isaiah." The

chapters beginning with Chapter Forty apparently belong to him, and their message was given at the time when Babylon fell.

The spiritual vision of this great prophet swept the tremendous happenings of his world. He saw Cyrus not as a new accident of history, but as the instrument of the Lord. The Holy One of Israel, to whom the nations were "as the small dust of the balance," who could bring princes to nothing and make the judges of the earth as vanity, was working out his redeeming purpose. So he brought to the exiles the thrilling word:

> Comfort, comfort my people,
>   says your God
> Speak tenderly to Jerusalem,
>   and cry to her
> that her warfare is ended,
>   that her iniquity is pardoned,
> that she has received from the Lord's hand
>   double for all her sins.
> Get you up to a high mountain,
>   O Zion, herald of good tidings;
> lift up your voice with strength,
>   O Jerusalem, herald of good tidings,
>   lift it up, fear not;
> say to the cities of Judah,
>   "Behold your God!"
> He will feed his flock like a shepherd,
>   he will gather the lambs in his arms,
> he will carry them in his bosom,
>   and gently lead those that are with young.

So also this great prophet of the end of the exile spoke and wrote of one who should be the servant of God's redeeming purpose through what he would endure. It may be that he was thinking of the exiles as "the servant"; it may be of some individual of his time; it may be of the Messiah who was to come.

> He was despised and rejected by men,
>   a man of sorrows and acquainted with grief.
> Surely he has borne our griefs
>   and carried our sorrows;

yet we esteemed him stricken,
smitten by God, and afflicted
But he was wounded for our transgressions,
he was bruised for our iniquities;
upon him was the chastisement that made us whole,
and with his stripes we are healed.

And whoever it may have been that the prophet was conceiving as "the servant," the prophecy he made is the immortal expression of the truth that it may be through suffering that life is purified and saved.

CHAPTER FORTY-SEVEN

Nehemiah Restores Jerusalem and Jewish Life

CYRUS AND his successors gave considerable freedom to the subject peoples. Jewish exiles were allowed to go back, if they chose, to Palestine. About the year 530 B.C. some of them did go back, and under Zerubbabel as civil leader, and Joshua as priest, they tried to build up again the life of Jerusalem. Zerubbabel was a descendant of Jehoiachin, the king who had been brought to Babylon with the captives. There was hope that once more the nation would be revived under the continued dynasty of David. But before long Zerubbabel disappeared, perhaps having fallen under the suspicion of Persia, and authority in Jerusalem was to center in the priests.

At first the returning exiles had all they could do in building houses for themselves amid the rubble of the city. Then there arose two men, Haggai and Zechariah, who were to be numbered among the prophets—though among the lesser ones. Both of them insisted that the first duty of the people was to rebuild the temple. At their urging, it was rebuilt. It was only a pathetic structure in comparison with the temple of Solomon which had been destroyed, but a symbol again of religious loyalty.

Many years went by, and Jerusalem was still no more than a shadow of the city it had once been. In 444 B.C. the Persian King was Artaxerxes, and at his court was a Jew named Nehemiah. Some who had straggled back from Jerusalem told Nehemiah of the city's desolation; and when he was in the king's presence his face was so sad that Artaxerxes asked him what was the matter.

Nehemiah told him, and Nehemiah begged that he might be allowed to go back to Jerusalem and see what he could do for its rebuilding.

Artaxerxes listened with favor; and he gave Nehemiah letters to the governors of the provinces through which he would pass, and also to the keeper of the king's forest, granting him timber for the work he wanted to do. So Nehemiah went on his way, and came to Jerusalem.

There he found what might well have turned him back dismayed. Under cover of the night he rode around the city, and what he saw were broken walls, and charred wood and ashes where once the gates had been. But Nehemiah had the courage of a man who believed that strength from God was working through him. The next day he called the people together. "You see the trouble we are in," he said, "how Jerusalem lies in ruins with its gates burned. Come, let us build the wall of Jerusalem, that we may no longer suffer disgrace."

His spirit kindled those who had had no spirit before. He organized all the able-bodied men of the city, divided them into working groups, and the rebuilding began. Not without difficulty and danger. There were some who circulated false rumors to undermine his leadership. There were hostile Arabs and Ammonites near Jerusalem who threatened attack; and a message was brought to Nehemiah stating that that night he would be assassinated unless he escaped by hiding in the temple. With a fine disdain he answered, "Should such a man as I flee? Go into the temple to save my life? I will not go in!" Nor did anyone finally dare to touch him. He kept on until the walls and the gates were restored, and he could say that even the hostile peoples round about "perceived that this work had been accomplished with the help of our God."

Nehemiah returned to Persia, as he had promised the king he would. But later he came back again to Jerusalem. This time Ezra, the scribe, was with him. They shared one absorbing purpose. It was all very well that Jerusalem was protected now from outside attack. But what of the life within it? It made little difference that the city should exist unless those who lived there showed themselves to be a people who remembered their covenant with God.

Ezra and Nehemiah gathered the whole assembly, and Ezra brought "the book of the law of Moses. He read from it facing the square before the Water Gate from early morning until mid day, in the presence of the men and women and those who could understand; and the ears of all the people were attentive to the book of the law." Then Ezra reviewed the long story of God's leading of his people, from the call of Abraham and the promise made to him; the deliverance from Egypt, and the revelation of God's word at Sinai. "Thou hast been just in all that has come upon us, for thou hast dealt faithfully and we have acted wickedly," said Ezra as he offered to God his prayer of confession for the people.

And the people were swept by an emotion of acknowledged guilt. They took an oath to obey henceforth the laws of God that had come through Moses, and to keep all the regulations that belonged to them as Jews. Nehemiah and Ezra made sternly plain what that oath included—circumcision, the strict keeping of the Sabbath and of all holy days, payments of their tithes and special offerings, and separation from all influences outside of Jewry. There were to be no more marriages with non-Jews, and mixed marriages already made should be broken up.

So there began a new period in Jewish history that would show magnificent fidelity, and at the same time a harshness that could be fanatical. The Jew must stand apart from all other peoples. In a world where the subtle influences of heathenism were everywhere, how else could he preserve the standards that gave moral greatness to his life? But the danger was that he might become self-righteous, and consider himself better than others because he shaped his behavior by more rigid religious forms. He would make his aloofness a matter of fierce pride, and thank God that he was not as other men are.

The most vivid witness in the scriptures to this conviction that the Jew and the world at large must stand in mortal conflict is the Book of Esther. Spiritual devotion and primitive racial passion are mingled in the dramatic story of a young queen whose courage saved her people.

Esther, the Jewess, is married to Ahasuerus, a despotic and capricious Persian king; but he does not know that she belongs to the Jewish people. The evil Haman, an officer in the king's court, hated Mordecai, Esther's cousin, because he thought Mordecai had not shown him enough respect; and he began an intrigue by which he hoped to bring about the death of Mordecai and of all who were connected with him. Through treacherous accusation he persuaded the king to issue an order "into all the king's provinces to destroy, to slay, and to annihilate all Jews, young and old, women and children, in one day, and to plunder their goods."

Now all the Jewish people stood in peril of their lives. Nothing could save them except a cancellation of the king's order; and no one had any chance of persuading the king to cancel it unless it should be the queen. Mordecai sent to her a desperate appeal. Would she go to Ahasuerus and plead with him against the evil purpose which Haman was trying to carry through? This might be her God-given opportunity. "Who knows," he said, "whether you have not come to the kingdom for such a time as this?"

"For such a time as this!" A dreadful time, and a frightful moment of decision, it seemed to the young girl queen. Ahasuerus had a temper that no one could predict. If she went to him and pleaded for the Jews, it might mean only that she herself would be put to death with the rest of her people.

But all the same she said that she would go. She begged Mordecai to gather together as many as he could to pray for her. And as to what might happen to her, pathetically, the only thing that she could say was "If I perish, I perish."

In her queenly robes she went then to the great hall where Ahasuerus sat on his royal throne, and she waited there before him while her heart stood still. What would Ahasuerus say and do?

What he did say made her heart begin to beat again. Her beauty and her gentleness changed whatever ugly mood he might have had. He asked her to tell him any request she had, and he would grant it.

She asked him to come, and to have Haman come, to a supper which she would prepare for the next evening. And Ahasuerus said it should be as she desired.

When Haman heard of that, he was filled with exultant pride. So he was to be the honor guest at the royal table! He went home and told his family all about it. He seemed to be so high in favor that he could look forward now to getting everything he wanted, including the thing he wanted most of all—the putting to death of Mordecai whom he hated. He would get ready for his day of vengeance. He had a gallows built; and he told himself that he could persuade the king to have Mordecai hanged upon it.

But that very night the king could not sleep. He ordered some records brought for him to read. In those records he read something which he had altogether forgotten—of how not long before he had been saved from possible death by a warning brought by Mordecai, the Jew—the warning of a plot of two conspirators to kill the king.

"What had been done to reward and honor Mordecai?" Ahasuerus asked. And the answer was that nothing had been done.

At that very moment who should come into the king's court but Haman; Haman, so sure of himself that he was ready to tell the king that it was time to send Mordecai to the gallows. Little did he know what the king had just been thinking.

"What ought to be done to a man whom the king wants to honor?" Ahasuerus said.

Here already—Haman thought—was his moment of triumph! Of course the king wanted to honor *him*. He would try to speak as though he did not guess that; but at the same time he would make sure that he would suggest the sort of honor that his pride desired most.

He answered that if the king wished to honor any man supremely, he might have him mounted on the king's own horse, dressed in royal robes, with a crown on his head; and some officer of the king should be ordered to lead the horse through the open square of the city, and proclaim there the man whom the king delighted to honor.

So it should be, Ahasuerus declared. He turned to Haman— "You go and do exactly what you have described," he said. "And the man I mean is Mordecai."

Then with strangled disgust and anger Hamen had to carry out the king's command. Instead of persuading the king to put Mordecai to death, he had to walk by the bridle of the horse on which Mordecai rode through the admiring city.

Nor was that the end of Haman's fall. The next evening came the queen's supper which he had thought would be another sign of how high he stood in the royal court. But before the supper was over the queen accused him to the king. "This wicked Haman," she said, had tried to turn the king against her people.

Ahasuerus rose up in wrath and strode out into the garden. The terrified Haman dropped down by the queen's couch to beg for mercy. Ahasuerus, coming back into the room, was furious to see him touch the queen. He called his servants, and they covered Haman's face as a sign that he was marked for death. One of them told the king of the gallows which Haman had already set up for Mordecai. "Take Haman out, and hang him on that," said Ahasuerus. And that is what they did.

So the one guilty man got the punishment he deserved. But the story in the Book of Esther does not end there. With the permission of the king, the Jews in all the provinces rose up to avenge themselves, and "smote all their enemies with the sword, slaughtering, and destroying them, and did as they pleased to those who hated them." Moreover, they made a feast of joy and gladness and established it as the annual festival of Purim, that the days of triumph over their enemies "should be remembered and kept throughout every generation."

CHAPTER FORTY-EIGHT

Judaism's Message to All Mankind

B UT ALONG with this fierce nationalism, so close to raw human instincts, there was a higher conception of the meaning of Jewry for the world. The Book of Jonah is an expression of it. In that Book the important parts are the beginning and the end, and not the middle which is most talked about. Jonah, the son of Amittai, is commanded by the Lord to go preach repentance to the hated city of Nineveh. He revolts from that idea. He will go in the opposite direction as far as he can. So he gets on board a ship going to "Tarshish," which probably means Tartessos in southern Spain, at the extreme end of the Mediterranean Sea.

Then comes the dramatic tale that puts in miraculous allegory the truth that God's sovereignty cannot be escaped. A great storm arises; Jonah's frightened conscience admits that this may be God's punishment for his disobedience; he is cast overboard into the sea; but a great fish swallows him and brings him back to land. Now Jonah has to go and preach in Nineveh, whether he wanted to or not.

Worst of all for his unwilling spirit, Ninevah listens and repents. As a Jew, the last thing that Jonah wanted was to have Nineveh be blessed by God. Sullen and resentful, he sits down for shelter on a burning hot day under a green plant. When it withered, he complained bitterly to God. Then the story comes to its climax— "God said to Jonah, 'Do you do well to be angry for the plant?' And he said, 'I do well to be angry, angry enough to die.' And the Lord said, 'You pity the plant, for which you did not labor, nor did you make it grow, which came into being in a night, and perished in a night. And should I not pity Nineveh, that great city, in which there are more than a hundred and twenty thousand persons who do not know their right hand from their left, and also much cattle?' "

So against the hardheartedness of Jonah there stands the compassion of God that reached out to the great city with its little
children, and even to the dumb beasts!

But most beautiful of all the Books as expressing kinship under
God with other peoples is the lovely little Book of Ruth.

In a time of famine, a family from Israel migrate into Moab—
the same Moab that was listed by the prophet Amos as one of the
peoples Israel hated most. But in the Book of Ruth the two sons
of the Israelitish family marry Moabite girls. The men die, and
their mother Naomi, a widow, will go back to Israel. She is leaving her daughters-in-law in their own land. But one of them,
Ruth, will not be separated. "Where you go, I will go," she said.
"Where you lodge, I will lodge; your people shall be my people,
and your God my God; where you die I will die, and there will I
be buried. May the Lord do so to me and more also if even death
parts me from you."

So Ruth came with Naomi into Israel. There she went out near
Bethlehem to glean grain in a field that belonged to a wealthy man
named Boaz. Boaz fell in love with her and they were married.
From that marriage a son, Obed, was born; and Obed was the
father of Jesse, who was the father of David. So in this Book of
Ruth there stood the everlasting reminder that the most beloved
of all the kings of Israel came from the motherhood of a Moabite
girl.

Also, there came from the midst of the Jewish people other
books that have become precious beyond the borders of any race
or nation. The books of the law were the ones that belonged most
particularly to the children of Abraham: books from Genesis
through Second Kings that told the long story of this people of
the covenant made at Sinai, of the Ten Commandments and the
other rules of life linked with the great name of Moses; books that
brought to every succeeding Jewish generation the reminder that
it belonged to "the Chosen People." Then there were the books
of the prophets which arose out of Jewish history but also had
their universal message. And finally there were the books which
the scribes who gathered up the records into the Hebrew Bible
called "the Writings."

To name them is to realize how wide their influence has been on the thought, the speech and the spiritual response of numberless human minds and souls.

There is "The Song of Songs," which is the celebration of an oriental wedding, with the lyrics of lovers one to another, full of the poetry of life at those moments when

> "lo, the winter is past,
>   the rain is over and gone.
> The flowers appear on the earth
>   and the time of the singing of birds has come."

There is the strange Book of Ecclesiastes, as to which one can be glad that it got into the Bible even though it seems so out of tune with the great central music of the Bible's faith. For it reflects a need in life which faith must deal with—the weary and disillusioned mood out of which may come the bitter question:

> "What does man gain by all the toil
>   at which he toils under the sun?
> A generation goes and a generation comes,
>   The sun rises and the sun goes down.
> All things are full of weariness;
>   a man cannot utter it;
> The eye is not satisfied with seeing,
>   nor the ear filled with hearing.
> What has been is what will be,
>   and what has been done is what will be done;
>   and there is nothing new under the sun.
> Vanity of vanities! All is vanity."

There is the Book of Proverbs, with its wisdom distilled from the ancient experience of many peoples. And there is the magnificent poetry of the Book of Job, that wrestles with the eternal problem of human suffering and the purpose of God that may be moving in the darkness where the sufferer cannot see.

But above all there is the Book of Psalms which has become the hymn book for a large part of the human race. In it souls of every sort have found the help they needed. There are the psalms that echo the cry of spiritual desire:

> Like as the hart desireth the water-brooks
> So longeth my soul after thee, O God
> My soul is athirst for God,
> Yea, even for the living God.

There are the psalms that speak from desolation, like the *De Profundis:*

> Out of the deep have I called unto thee, O Lord
> Lord, hear my voice!

There are the confessions of sin and the voice of penitence:

> Have mercy upon me, O God, after thy great goodness
> According to the multitude of thy mercies do away my offenses.

There are the psalms of praise and thanksgiving:

> O come let us sing unto the Lord,
>   let us heartily rejoice in the strength of our salvation

And perhaps best remembered and loved among them all is the 23rd Psalm with its word of final trust:

> The Lord is my shepherd;
>   Therefore can I lack nothing.

Thus in the Book of Psalms, as well as in much else of the Bible, the spirit of Jewry went out to find contact with all mankind.

CHAPTER FORTY-NINE

The Flame
of Undying Courage

B UT ALTHOUGH Israel could thus recognize that it had ties to
the wide human family, the relentless facts of history compelled the people to increasing separateness as the price for their
survival.

In the final third of the fourth century B.C., the conquests of
Alexander the Great had spread the influence of Greece across the
world. There was danger that Greek ideas, Greek philosophy, and
the mingling of religions which had followed the conquests of
Alexander might stifle the Jewish witness to the Holy One of
Israel. That danger became acute in the second century B.C., when
Alexander's empire had been divided, and Antiochus Epiphanes,
king of Syria, ruled over Palestine. He represented all that was
worst in the so-called culture of the time—its luxury, its lack of
principle, its contempt for lofty standards of belief and of behavior. He saw the religion of the Jews as a stubborn barrier to
conformity in his kingdom. So he set out to destroy it. He ordered
all books of the law to be surrendered and burned. He defiled the
temple at Jerusalem and set up a heathen altar in it. And he sent
armed officers to hunt down every Jew who would not bow to his
corrupting purpose.

But now began an era which was to be a witness to a devotion
in the heart of Israel that made Israel fit to be a special people in
the sight of God. Among the hills of Judah lived a man of a priestly
family, named Mattathias. One day when a Syrian officer was demanding of the Jews that they offer pagan sacrifice, Mattathias
answered, "Though all the nations that are under the king's

203

dominion obey him and fall away every one from the religion of their fathers, yet will I and my sons and my brethren walk in the covenant of our fathers. God forbid that we should forsake the law and the ordinances. We will not hearken to the king's words, to go from our religion, either on the right hand or on the left."

And not in speech only did Mattathias make his defiance. When a Jew moved forward to obey the Syrian's command to sacrifice, Mattathias struck him down. Then he killed the Syrian also, and he and his sons sounded a call to revolt that spread like fire through Israel.

They were engaged in what might have seemed a hopeless struggle—men rallying from anywhere and nowhere to make a fighting force that could dare attack the organized Syrian army. But under Mattathias' son, Judas—Judas Maccabaeus, or "the Hammerer"—and under the next son, Simon, when Judas had been killed, the Syrian control was actually broken, the Temple cleansed, and men in Judah made free again to worship according to the religion of their fathers. The men who fought under the banner of the Maccabees lived up to the charge that Mattathias gave before he died—"Be zealous for the law, and give your lives for the covenants of your fathers. Fear not the words of a sinful man. Today he shall be lifted up, and tomorrow he shall not be found, because he is returned to dust, and his thought is come to nothing. Wherefore, my sons, be valiant!"

And the strength on which they relied, and which made them valiant, was expressed in the answer Judas Maccabaeus gave to his men in a moment of great danger. "How shall we be able, being so few, to fight against so great a multitude and so strong?" they asked him. And he said, "It is no hard matter for many to be shut up in the hands of a few! And with the God of heaven it is all one, to deliver with a great multitude or a small company; for the battle standeth not in the multitude of an host; but strength cometh from heaven."

The state that the Maccabees re-established fell apart again. In the years to come the Jews would suffer under many rulers. The importance among the nations which was linked with the memory of the kingdom of David and Solomon was gone. But a religious community was being shaped, which would outlast many earthly sovereignties. For more than two thousand years after Antiochus Epiphanes lived and died the Jews would continue—and have continued—to carry the flame of witness to the God of righteousness and truth.

In evil times as well as good, there was one great standard around which their life could rally. They had the law and the message of the prophets, so that even when their way led through the darkness they could say, "Thy word is a lantern to my feet, and a light upon my paths."

At the time of the persecution under Antiochus Epiphanes there was need of every message that would reinforce the people's faith. So to the rest of what made up the Holy Book there was added now the prophesy called the Book of Daniel. The name of Daniel —though only his name—had appeared in the prophesy of Ezekiel, as a man conspicuous in righteousness. Around him heroic stories had grown up, and in the Book of Daniel these stories were brought together, along with burning prophesies and visions of the awful purposes of God. Here men could read how tyranny had been resisted before, and tyrants made to acknowledge a power greater than their earthly threats.

Daniel is described as one of the captives brought to Babylon, and by his wisdom having won the favor of Nebuchadnezzar, the king. He interprets a dream of Nebuchadnezzar, and the king is grateful. He makes Daniel ruler of one of the provinces of Babylon; and he gives positions of honor also to three friends of Daniel —Shadrach, Meshach and Abednego.

But now comes a different story. Nebuchadnezzar set up a great golden image on the plain of Dura, and ordered a magnificent ritual of worship of the gods of Babylon. When the sound of the cornets and other massed music began, the crowds were to fall on their faces in obeisance to the image. So they did—all except three men; and those three were Daniel's friends, Shadrach, Meshach and Abednego.

Then was Nebuchadnezzar full of rage! He ordered those three brought before him. Was it true that they had refused to bow down before the image? Yes, it was true, they said. And so they had defied him! The furious king would give them one more chance. When the music began again, if they did not bow down and worship he would have them thrown into a blazing furnace; "and who is the god," he said, "that will deliver you out of my hands?"

Shadrach, Meshach and Abednego answered the king—"O Nebuchadnezzar, we have no need to answer you in this matter. If it be so, our God whom we serve is able to deliver us from the burning fiery furnace; and he will deliver us out of your hand, O king. *But if not,* be it known unto you, O king, that we will not serve your gods or worship the golden image which you have set up!"

"Heat the furnace seven times hotter than it was before!" Nebuchadnezzar commanded. And into the furnace, their hands and feet bound, Shadrach, Meshach and Abednego were thrown.

The king sat on his throne and watched to see them consumed. Then suddenly he stood up in amazement. "Three men were thrown into the furnace," he exclaimed. "True, O King," those around him answered. "But I see *four* men loose," he said, "walking in the midst of the fire, and they are not hurt, and the appearance of the fourth is like a son of the gods."

So the awed king came near to the door of the furnace. "Shadrach, Meshach and Abednego, servants of the Most High God, come forth," he said, "and come here!"

Then out of the furnace they came, unhurt, with no scar from fire or smell of smoke about them. Whereupon, as the climax to the triumphant story, Nebuchadnezzar made his own confession— "Blessed be the Lord God of Shadrach, Meshach and Abednego, who has sent his angel and delivered his servants, who trusted in him, and set at nought the king's command, and yielded up their bodies rather than serve and worship any god except their own God."

But according to the traditions that echoed in the Book of Daniel, Nebuchadnezzar was to be humbled before the sovereignty of God in a shocking way. Walking one day on the roof of the royal palace, he looked with haughty pride upon the grandeur of walls and streets and temples spread out beneath his gaze. "This is great Babylon," he said, "which I have built by my mighty power and for the glory of my majesty."

While the words were still in the king's mouth, there fell a voice from heaven, "O king Nebuchadnezzar, to you it is spoken: the kingdom has departed from you, and you shall be driven from among men, and your dwelling shall be with the beasts of the field; and you shall be made to eat grass like an ox; and seven times shall pass over you, until you have learned that the Most High rules the kingdom of men and gives it to whom he will."

So, like a creature demented, Nebuchadnezzar went out to wander in the fields, until his reason returned to him. And when it did, he blessed the Most High and praised and honored him who lives forever—"for his dominion is an everlasting dominion, and his kingdom endures from generation to generation."

CHAPTER FIFTY

The Eternal Hope

THEN IN the Book of Daniel the scene and the time move on. Now the king is Belshazzar, Nebuchadnezzar's son.

Belshazzar made a great feast for a thousand of his lords; and as they began to drink wine Belshazzar commanded that the gold and silver chalices which had been taken out of the Temple in Jerusalem should be brought for his concubines to drink from.

Then came a sight that struck the king and his company cold with dread. A great hand appeared, and began to write on the wall of the banquet hall. "Bring in the enchanters and the astrologers," the king cried. They came, but they could not read the words that the hand was writing.

Now Daniel was summoned. The king offered him a rich reward if he could interpret what was written. "Give your rewards to another," Daniel said, but he would tell him the meaning of the inscription. *Mene, mene, tekel upharsin,* were the grim words which the hand had traced. And this is what they meant for this king who had blasphemously drunk his wine from the chalices looted from the temple:

> God has numbered the days of your kingdom and brought it to an end.
> You have been weighed in the balances and found wanting.
> Your kingdom is divided and given to the Medes and Persians.

That night Belshazzar the king of Babylon was slain; and Darius the Mede ruled in his place.

Thus the tale of triumph over tyrannies extends its scope, from the days of Babylon to the days of the Persian empire that succeeded it; and it comes to its climax with the story of Daniel in the lions' den.

Lords in the kingdom who were jealous of Daniel began to plot together how they might destroy him. They knew that in his house there was an upper room with windows opening toward Jerusalem, and there three times a day Daniel knelt down with his eyes toward what had been the Holy City and prayed to his fathers' God. Then his enemies persuaded the king to issue an order that no one in the kingdom should dare make appeal to any power other than the king. When the decree was signed and sealed they told the king of Daniel and his daily habit of praying to his fathers' God.

The king admired Daniel and had no wish to harm him, but he was caught in his own commitment. He could not withdraw the decree which he had issued. So Daniel was thrust into a pit where the king kept uncaged lions.

At daybreak the next day Darius came to the edge of the pit and cried in a voice of anguish, "O Daniel, servant of the living God, has your God, whom you serve continually, been able to save you from the lions?" Back came the voice of Daniel saying that the Lord had shut the lions' mouths and no hurt had come to him. So Daniel was taken out of the lions' den, one more among the heroic souls who had dared to trust in God.

From the stories of the past that had grown in their telling and re-telling, the Book of Daniel moves on in its final chapters to the great visions which dramatized the invincible faith of Jewry for all the years ahead. In those visions the tyrannous earthly kingdoms rise like beasts from the earth, but one by one the beasts are caged or slain. "And, behold, with the clouds of heaven

> There came one like a son of man,
> and he came to the Ancient of Days
>   and was presented before him.
> And to him was given dominion
>   and glory and kingdom,
> that all peoples, nations and languages
>   should serve him;
> his dominion is an everlasting dominion,
>   which shall not pass away,
> and his kingdom one
>   that shall not be destroyed.

So for the Jewish people there was voiced the shining conviction that the Deliverer would come. The kingdoms of this earth might flourish for a while, but the final sovereignty belonged to God. That is why through all the centuries this people of the Covenant, often persecuted, sometimes homeless, have moved on their eternal road toward the deathless hope, written in the Book of Malachi which brings the Old Testament to its end, that in God's good time "the sun of righteousness shall arise with healing in his wings."

Index